Prepare your Heart

Scripture Readings
and
Reflections
for

Advent

Alonso de Blas, OFM

TAU

Prepare your Heart
Scripture Readings and Reflections for Advent

Alonso de Blas, OFM

© 2008 Tau Publishing

Book and cover design: Tau Publishing Design Dept.
Cover image: I-Stock Photo

For permission contact:
Tau Publishing, LLC
Permissions Dept.
1422 East Edgemont Avenue
Phoenix, AZ 85006

Second Edition, 2011
10 9 8 7 6 5 4 3 2
ISBN: 978-1-935257-40-0

Published by Tau Publishing, LLC
www.Tau-Publishing.com
Printed in the United States of America.

Tau-Publishing.com

Words and Works of Inspiration

*For my brother friars who
are now resting in Paradise with
our Lord.*

INTRODUCTION

The word Advent means "coming," in Church use, the coming of Christ our Savior. There are many ways Christ comes to us. The most obvious, speaking of the Season of Advent, is his birth at Bethlehem some 2000 years ago. But once Christmas is over, we can also think pretty naturally of the coming of Christ at the Parousia, the end of time, when he'll return on the clouds in power and majesty to bring into order all creation and place it once more in the Creator's loving hands.

Then too, in our everyday devotional lives, we pray for the coming of Jesus more deeply into our hearts, and we invite this renewed presence by turning to him in prayer, in spiritual reading, in apostolic activity, but most especially in the reception of Holy Communion at the Eucharist.

Not surprisingly, the Church's celebration of Advent capitalizes on all these ways to spot the Lord's coming to us, by helping us to prepare for, to pay attention to, and to make room for his coming. Especially in the liturgical readings of the season we recall the many promises of help that God extended through the prophets of the Old Testament to his people as they languished in Exile, feeling abandoned while acknowledging their guilt and their need for his rescue. Then in the Gospels we find the fulfillment of all those hints and promises, and share in the joy of the arrival of God's long-awaited rescue. God's promised Messiah has come and saved us, but it is an ongoing process to which we are called to contribute. So we look back to our helplessness before Jesus came into our lives, and we look forward to his glorious return to lead us to heaven. But we are also called to attention to the present moment, to not miss the many ways in which we encounter, and in fact can bring to each other, his saving grace and loving, forgiving presence. Is it just by chance that we always picture Mary not washing her hair or rinsing the dishes, but quietly at prayer, when she is visited by the angel Gabriel?

FIRST SUNDAY OF ADVENT
Cycle A – Scripture:

Isaiah 2:1-5 *In days to come, / the mountain of the Lord's house / shall be established as the highest mountain / and raised above the hills. / All nations shall stream toward it; / many peoples shall come and say: / "Come, let us climb the Lord's mountain, / that he may instruct us in his ways, / and we may walk in his paths." / He shall judge between the nations, / and impose terms on many peoples. / They shall beat their swords into plowshares / and their spears into pruning hooks; / one nation shall not raise the sword against another, / nor shall they train for war again. / O house of Jacob, come, / let us walk in the light of the Lord.*

Responsorial Psalm 122: 1-2, 3-4, 4-5, 6-7, 8-9

Romans 13: 11-14 *It is now the hour for you to wake from sleep, for our salvation is closer than when we first accepted the faith. The day draws near. Let us cast off deeds of darkness and put on the armor of light.*

Matthew 24: 37-44 Jesus reminds his followers how in the days of Noah people kept eating and drinking and carrying on right up to the day of the flood. Since they were totally taken up with the cares of their daily life, they missed the boat! *"Stay awake, therefore!*

You cannot know the day your Lord is coming." In fact, *"the Son of Man is coming at the time you least expect."*

Reflection:

When Yahweh's kingdom arrives, it will be centered on his holy mountain, and will draw <u>all</u> people from the world over. His chosen will set the pace and model his instructions, and all shall embrace peace. Now is the time to respond to the call to end wars and hostility, and to begin to live like brothers, in the light, honorably, led by Christ's example. The gospel cannot be any clearer: he's on his way to us, let's stay awake and watch and prepare for his coming by taking on his way of life—now!

FIRST SUNDAY OF ADVENT
Cycle B – Scripture

Isaiah 63: *16-17, 19; 64:2-7 You, Lord, are our father, / our redeemer forever. / Return for the sake of your servants. / Rend the heavens and come down / with the mountains quaking before you. / Our guilt carries us away like the wind. / There is none who calls upon your name, / who rouses himself to cling to you. / For you have hidden your face from us / and have delivered us up to our guilt. / Yet, O Lord, you are our father; / we are the clay and you are the potter; / we are all the work of your hands.*

Responsorial Psalm 80: 2-3, 15-16, 18-19

1 Corinthians 1:3-9 *You lack no spiritual gift as you wait for the revelation of our Lord Jesus. You will be blameless on the day of our Lord Jesus Christ. God is faithful, and it was he who called you to fellowship with his Son.*

Mark 13: 33-37 *Jesus said to his disciples: "Be constantly on the watch! Stay awake! You do not know when the master of the house is coming. Do not let him come suddenly and catch you asleep. What I say to you, I say to all: be on guard!"*

Reflection:
(Second) Isaiah's selection is chock-full of Advent bits: our awareness of our sin and therefore of our need for a redeemer, the powerful picture of God rending the heavens and coming to our rescue, the confidence of being clay in the potter's hands, so that he can do as he wills with us, since we remain the work of his hands.

This is echoed in Paul's image of us, waiting for the revelation of our Lord Jesus Christ to make itself ever more manifest in us, making us blameless at the day of his coming. And we can be sure of it, because it is our faithful God who calls us to fellowship with his son. And Mark catches Jesus' urgency as he goes almost non-stop, getting his listeners ready to spot and accept the reign of God approaching in his person: Heads up! Watch for it! Don't miss it!

First Sunday of Advent

Cycle C – Scripture

Jeremiah 33:14-16 *The days are coming, says the LORD, when I will fulfill the promise I made to the house of Israel and Judah. In those days, in that time, I will raise up for David a just shoot; he shall do what is right and just in the land. In those days Judah shall be safe and Jerusalem shall dwell secure; this is what they shall call her: "The LORD our justice."*

Responsorial Psalm 122: 1-2, 3-4, 4-5, 6-7, 8-9

First Thessalonians 3:12-4:2 *May the Lord make you increase in love so as to strengthen your hearts, to be blameless in holiness before our God and Father at the coming of our Lord Jesus. We exhort you in the Lord Jesus that, as you received from us how you should conduct yourselves to please God—and as you are conducting yourselves—you do so even more.*

Luke 21:25-28, 34-36 *And then they will see the Son of Man coming in a cloud with power and great glory. But when these signs begin to happen, stand erect and raise your heads because your redemption is at hand.*

Reflection:

Jeremiah makes clear our reason for renewed hope even as the world around us almost suffocates us with bad news, upheavals, suffering and constant anxiety. The Lord has promised to raise up for us a just shoot, a new start in the almost-dead stump of David's once-flowering tree, his royal lineage in the house of Israel and Judah. "In those days Judah shall be safe and Jerusalem shall dwell secure." God makes himself the pledge of our future safety.

In the Gospel, Jesus speaks of the coming of God's power on that last and frightful day when heaven and earth will be shaken as the Son of Man comes "in a cloud with power and great glory." The sun, the moon, the seas and the earth will be in great disarray, and fear will come over all. All our plans, our expectations, the very ground beneath us will come to a crashing halt…what's happening? Jesus calms us, as he once calmed the frightened disciples in the boat tossed by the waves: "when these things begin to happen, stand erect and raise your heads, because your redemption is at hand."

That last day, the parousia, is the end of the reign of sin and death, of a world that is a place of suffering, imperfect, unfair, out of whack. It is the beginning of the reign of God's peace and love, of forgiveness and complete understanding. They shall call the new Jerusalem "The Lord our Justice." God himself will wipe away our tears and calm our fears. Can you see a mother picking up her distraught young child who has let go of her hand and now, frightened at losing sight of her in a crowd, calls out for her in panic?

So, do we have to wait till the end of the world to experience our salvation? St. Paul writes to the Christians at Thessalonika, praying that the Lord will make them grow in love, so they may be "blameless in holiness before our God and Father at the coming of the Lord Jesus" at the end of time. But he also exhorts them to continue to conduct themselves to please God, even as they are doing now, but even more. That Lord Jesus who will come in glory and power on the last day to make things right is the same Jesus who came to us at Bethlehem, to walk with us and show us the way to please God, to invite us and empower us to help him spread his Father's kingdom of peace and love.

To prepare for his coming in glory we first look back to his humble coming to us at Christmas, as that tiny new shoot, a new growth of hope for a weary world. God's final victory is assured, and it has already begun—we celebrate it with our yearly gathering around the crib of his beloved Son, our brother in human flesh and condition, our leader into his risen life beyond our graves. Good news! Mary's pregnant with the hope promised by our saving God!

MONDAY FIRST WEEK

Scripture

Isaiah 2:1-5 *In days to come, / the mountain of the LORD'S house / shall be established as the highest mountain / and raised above the hills. / All nations shall stream toward it; / many peoples shall come and say: / "Come, let us climb the LORD'S mountain, / to the house of the God of Jacob, / that he may instruct us in his ways, / and we may walk in his paths." / They shall beat their swords into plowshares / and* *their spears into pruning hooks; / one nation shall not raise the sword against another, / nor shall they train for war again.*

Responsorial Psalm 122: 1-2, 3-4, 4-5. 6-7, 8-9

Matthew 8:5-11 *"Lord, only say the word and my servant will be healed." When Jesus heard this, he was amazed and said to those following him, "Amen, I say to you, in no one in Israel have I found such faith."*

Reflection:
Remember Jeremiah quoting God "in those days"? First thing out of Isaiah's mouth in today's reading again has us look to the <u>parousia</u>, the last day, when God will make all things right for his people: "In days to come, the mountain of the Lord's house shall be established as the highest mountain and raised above the hills." The Temple mount in Jerusalem will stand out, so that all its people, and those beyond, will see the house of God and be drawn to it to be instructed in His ways.

And what beautiful instruction they'll receive! As a result, they will train for war no more. They won't raise the sword against each other again; in fact, they'll turn their spears into pruning hooks. What a wonderful development—from the art of war to finer homes and gardens. From looking to harm to looking to feed...does this sound topical enough for our world still today? Think of the military and weaponry industry and then consider the task for the little groups of people dedicated to finding and removing the untold thousands of landmines dotting abandoned fields of battle and still threatening innocent farmers and travelers. Just because it's Vietnam and not some Pennsylvania Civil War site doesn't mean we can ignore it.

In the Gospel Jesus warns against complacency: "we're special because we're Catholics." He marvels at the faith shown by the centurion, a Gentile, who doesn't need to have Jesus present at his boy's bedside. If Jesus decides to heal him from right here, that'll do. He can believe it without seeing Jesus doing it, and he's not even a fellow Jew! The lesson: don't count on just the label Christian to make you OK. Get busy and come to the Lord's mountain and follow His instruction so you can live and not just claim the Christian life.

TUESDAY FIRST WEEK

Scripture

Isaiah 11:1-10 *A shoot shall sprout from the stump of Jesse, / and from his roots a bud shall blossom. / The spirit of the LORD shall rest upon him: / a spirit of wisdom and of understanding, / a spirit of counsel and of strength, / a spirit of knowledge and of fear of the LORD. / He shall judge the poor with justice, / and decide aright for the land's afflicted. / Then the wolf shall be a guest of the lamb, / and the leopard shall lie down with the kid; / the calf and the young lion shall browse together, / with a little child to guide them. / There shall be no harm or ruin on all my holy mountain. / The root of Jesse, / set up as a signal for the nations, / the Gentiles shall seek out, / for his dwelling shall be glorious.*

Responsorial Psalm 72:1, 7-8, 12-13, 17

Luke 10:21-24 *"I give you praise, Father, Lord of heaven and earth, for although you have hidden these things from the wise and the learned you have revealed them to the childlike." Turning to the disciples in private he said, "Blessed are the eyes that see what you see."*

Reflection:
From Isaiah comes one of the most beautiful Emmanuel prophecies. Once more, "on that day," a bud shall blossom from the roots of the unlikely remains of the "stump of Jesse" (King David's father). "The spirit of the Lord shall rest upon him," with a lower-case S, meaning he is enlivened, inspired by the Lord, but the listing of the virtues is a clear catalog of what we have come to know as the Gifts of the Holy Spirit,

with a capital S. What a champion we have, coming to our rescue, striking the ruthless and slaying the wicked, but judging the poor with justice, and deciding aright for the afflicted.

In the gospel Jesus praises the Father for revealing to him and to the other little ones what the smart, clever people cannot fathom: that the poor will be lifted out of their misery, the outcasts will be invited in, sinners and backsliders will be offered another chance to come close, that the little ones, passed over by the world, are important to God!

Hard to believe, isn't it? It hardly makes sense. But remember Isaiah's re-phrasing? When Jesus tells his disciples privately: "Blest are the eyes that see what you see," we picture Isaiah's scene presented so tenderly, with a child-like appeal that is pure Disney, a natural for children's coloring books or a quilt for their beds. The calf and the lion cub are joined at play by a little child romping. And instead of the wolf having the lamb over for dinner (burp), "the wolf shall be a guest of the lamb." To sum up, "there shall be no harm or ruin on all my holy mountain," says the Lord, and in the words of Isaiah "his dwelling shall be glorious." Amen. Let the day come!

WEDNESDAY FIRST WEEK

Scripture

Isaiah 25:6-10 *On this mountain the LORD of hosts / will provide for all peoples / a feast of rich food and choice wines, / juicy, rich food and pure, choice wines. / On that day it will be said: / "Behold our God, to whom we looked to save us!"*

Responsorial Psalm 23: 1-3, 3-4, 5, 6

Matthew 15:29-37 *Great crowds came to him, having with them the lame, the blind, the deformed, the mute, and many others. They placed* *them at his feet, and he cured them. " My heart is moved with pity for the crowd, for they have been with me now for three days and have nothing to eat."*

Reflection:

Isaiah today takes us from chronology ("on this day") to geography ("on this mountain"). Mount Zion, which has witnessed a multitude of reversals and threats to the safety of Jerusalem, and even the disastrous defeat, devastation, and deportation by the forces of Babylon which comes after Isaiah's death, is God's chosen site for his victory banquet when all foes are finally vanquished. God will provide for all peoples (Jews and Gentiles alike) a feast of rich food and choice wines, as any contemporary menu would proudly print, "juicy, rich food and pure, choice wines."

Matthew's good news reports Jesus curing cripples, the deformed, the blind, the mute, and many others the crowds brought and laid at his feet, much to their grateful astonishment. Even the healthy ones are targets of Jesus' concern, for now, after three days with him, they have nothing to eat. This miraculous feeding (of the four thousand) follows the first miracle of the loaves and fishes (for five thousand customers) in the previous chapter. (And it's interesting that only Mark, in his 8th chapter, reports likewise this second miraculous feeding.) Anyway, there it is, a sneak preview of the Messianic Banquet that God will provide for all his children at the great gathering beyond time.

And how can we know this? Because Isaiah assures us that "on this mountain" ["on that day"] the Lord will destroy death forever. On that day we'll be able to say "Behold our God—look at Him, here He is!" The One we've been counting on has come to save us!

Thursday First Week

Scripture

Isaiah 26:1-6 *Trust in the LORD forever! / For the LORD is an eternal Rock.*

Responsorial Psalm 118:1, 8-9, 19-21, 25-27

Matthew 7:21, 24-27 *Everyone who listens to these words of mine but does not act on them will be like a fool who built his house on sand.*

Reflection:

God is my Rock, my Fortress, the source of my strength and confidence when I find myself in trouble or discover I'm all alone in this mess. The ones on whom I counted are all gone; it's just me and God…. I've often wondered why, in the movies, when the pilot steps out of the cockpit to tell the passengers "The controls are all dead; we're in the hands of God now" they all gasp and shriek. When you think about it, in whose hands are you safer—the pilot's or God's? (Of course, at a time like that, who has time to get analytical?)

In the closing words of his Sermon on the Mount, Jesus makes the powerful contrast that appears in today's gospel selection. Just to hear the words of Jesus but not put them into practice is no guarantee of success. It's like building on sand, which can shift or melt away in a storm. Our ultimate security against the adversities of life is to listen to Jesus and then put his words into practice in our lives, so that God becomes the rock foundation on which we stand in safety no matter what comes. As Isaiah exhorts us: "Trust in the Lord forever, for the Lord is an eternal rock."

P.S. For extra credit, you might want to look up 1Cor. 10:4 for St. Paul's allusion to an old Jewish pious tradition, which my good old Jerusalem Bible explains in a footnote, and which is explained in greater detail in the New American Bible's footnote on the same verse.

IMMACULATE CONCEPTION OF THE BLESSED VIRGIN MARY

Scripture

Genesis 3:9-15, 20 *I will put enmity between you and the woman, and between your offspring and hers; he will strike at your head, while you strike at his heel."*

Responsorial Psalm 98:1, 2-3, 3-4

Ephesians 1:3-6, 11-12 *He chose us in him, before the foundation of the world, to be holy and without blemish before him. In love he destined us for adoption to himself through Jesus Christ.*

Luke 1:26-38 *The angel said to her, "Do not be afraid, Mary, for you have found favor with God. The Holy Spirit will come upon you, and the power of the Most High will overshadow you." Mary said, "Behold, I am the handmaid of the Lord. May it be done to me according to your word."*

Reflection:

From the moment Mary was conceived in the womb of her mother, St. Anne, God was preparing her for a choice she would face in her teen years. She would be offered, as we read in today's gospel, the invitation to set aside all her own plans for her future and to accept God's plan for her to become the mother of his Son on earth.

If she were to agree to do so, it would be only fitting for her to be preserved from any and all contact with sin, so her body and soul, her whole person, could be a fit vessel for the wonderful gift of God's living Son growing within her. The Church's traditional explanation of the appearance of evil in a world which God created as good, is based on today's selection from Genesis: we are tempted by the devil's appeal to our pride, and we fall prey to his trick as we disobey our loving Creator's design for our wellbeing, by not depending on Him and all He provides for us in that splendid Garden of Eden.

Following St. Augustine, the Church taught that Original Sin, our inherited tendency to weakness, to being duped by the devil's temptations, was passed on in our human nature in the natural physical production of our bodies. So God steps in to keep Mary's body unstained, immaculate, from the moment its production begins. That way his Son would remain totally faithful to his holy divine nature even as he undertook life in our human nature.

But even as our Just God pronounces our sentence of banishment, our Loving Creator gives us our first reason for hope in this battle between humanity and the devil: the woman's offspring "will strike at your head while you strike at his heel." Since the time of the earliest commentators this scriptural passage (Gen. 3:15) has been called the protoevangelion, the first good news.

As Paul reminds the Christians at Ephesus, we too are chosen, predestined to become God's adopted children, by the divine favor of our rebirth in the Holy Spirit as brothers and sisters of Jesus, "to be holy and blameless [spotless] in his sight, to be full of love." Is there a better description of what we become every time we receive the Eucharist and carry within us, as Mary did, God's living Son?

FRIDAY FIRST WEEK

Scripture

Isaiah 29: 17-24 *On that day the deaf shall hear, / and the eyes of the blind shall see. / The lowly will ever find joy in the Lord, / and the poor rejoice in the Holy One of Israel. / Jacob shall have nothing to be ashamed of, / when his children see / the work of my hands in his midst, / they shall reverence the Holy One of Jacob, / and be in awe of the God of Israel.*

Responsorial Psalm 27: 1, 4, 13-14

Matthew 9: 27-31 *Jesus said to the two blind men, "Are you confident I can do this?" "Yes, Lord," they told him. At that he touched their eyes and said, "Because of your faith it shall be done to you," and they recovered their sight.*

Reflection:
Jesus fulfills Isaiah's prophecy—the blind receive their sight! Remember when Jesus' message is being rejected by the Pharisees, and he gets exasperated with them and says, OK, so don't put any faith in my words—how about my works? Can't you see me doing the Father's saving work? Let them convince you to pay attention to me, because what I say is not from me, but from the Father who sent me.

SATURDAY FIRST WEEK

Scripture

Isaiah 30:19-21, 23-26 *O people of Zion, / no more will you weep; / He will be gracious to you when you cry out, / as soon as he hears he will answer you. / No longer will your Teacher hide himself. / From behind,* *a voice shall sound in your ears: / "This is the way; walk in it," / when you would turn to the right or to the left. / On the day the LORD binds up the wounds of his people, / he will heal the bruises left by his blows.*

Responsorial Psalm 147: 1-2, 3-4, 5-6

Matthew 9:35--10:1, 6-8 *Jesus went around to all the towns and villages, teaching in their synagogues, proclaiming the gospel of the kingdom, and curing every disease and illness. At the sight of the crowds, his heart was moved with pity for them because they were troubled and abandoned, like sheep without a shepherd. "Go to the lost sheep of the house of Israel. As you go, make this proclamation: 'The kingdom of heaven is at hand.' Without cost you have received; without cost you are to give."*

Reflection:

After Jerusalem survived the Assyrian threat that brought down the Kingdom of Israel (the ten northern tribes) in 721 BC, Isaiah reassures its inhabitants "no more will you weep." God will hear you and answer you when you cry out to Him. "No longer will your Teacher hide himself, but with your own eyes you shall see your Teacher." When you would turn to the right or to the left (to go your own way, as the hapless tribes of the northern kingdom had, to their ruin), you will hear a voice pointing out the right way. And finally, "on the day the Lord binds up the wounds of his people, he will heal the bruises left by his blows."

We find these words fulfilled in today's gospel. Wherever he goes, Jesus teaches in the synagogues, proclaims the good news, and cures every sickness and disease. He is moved by the plight of the crowds, who are like sheep without shepherds. So he sends his twelve disciples, giving them authority to "expel unclean spirits and to cure sickness and disease of every kind." And their target is the lost sheep of the house of Israel. "As you go, make this announcement: 'The reign of God is at hand!'"

Can we leave Mass expecting God's kingdom to simply come to us, without following up on the commission: "Go in peace to love and serve the Lord, to spread the news of God's Kingdom"? And what's our target—the people next to us in church, or the people who don't come to church with us and are lost and wandering, and wondering if there is a God, if they are loved, if their lives have meaning? The love God gives you unearned, share with others at your own expense.

SECOND SUNDAY OF ADVENT
Cycle A – Scripture

Isaiah 11: 1-10 *On that day, a shoot shall sprout from the stump of Jesse, / and from his roots a bud shall blossom. / The spirit of the Lord shall rest upon him. / He shall judge the poor with justice, / and decide aright for the land's afflicted. / On that day, / the root of Jesse, / set up as a signal for the nations, / the Gentiles shall seek out.*

Responsorial Psalm 72: 1-2, 7-8, 12-13, 17

Romans 15: 4-9 *Christ became the servant of the Jews because of God's faithfulness in fulfilling the promises to the patriarchs whereas the Gentiles glorify God because of his mercy.*

Matthew 3: 1-12 John the Baptist appears at the Jordan, preaching a baptism for the forgiveness of sins, Isaiah's "voice in the desert: Prepare the way of the Lord!" He announces the arrival of one more powerful: he will baptize not in water, but in the Holy Spirit and fire. He will gather the grain into the barn, but will set fire to the chaff.

Reflection:
In Isaiah's prophecy we have the description of a Davidic descendant (Jesse is David's father) upon whom God's spirit will rest and through

whom God's spirit will work. [There is a Disneyesque vision of voracious animals—all as cute little cubs—getting along famously with each other and with a human "cub," a little trusting child. This new king will do away with all enmities!]

More to the point, the Gentiles will flock to this king whom God has set up as a signal for the nations, not just for his fellow Jews. Paul follows up succinctly: in sending us this Messiah, God is being faithful to his ancient promises to the Chosen People, but he sends him to the whole rest of the world, too (the Gentiles), not because of any promises to them, but simply to show his great mercy toward all his people. Any pointers we might pick up from this moving, beyond loyalty owed, to mercy graciously offered?

Matthew's Baptist shares his cousin Jesus' urgency about making ready for the kingdom's arrival into your life. "Even now the axe is laid to the root of the tree. Every tree that is not fruitful will be cut down and thrown into the fire."

SECOND SUNDAY OF ADVENT
Cycle B – Scripture

Isaiah 40: 1-5, 9-11 *Comfort my people, says your God. / Speak tenderly to Jerusalem, and proclaim to her / that her guilt is expiated. / In the desert prepare the way of the Lord! / Make straight in the wasteland a highway for our God! / Every valley shall be filled in, / every mountain and hill shall be made low. / Then the glory of the Lord shall be revealed / and all mankind shall see it together. / Here is your God! / Here comes with power the Lord God / who rules by his strong arm. / Like a shepherd he feeds his flock; / in his arms he gathers the lambs, / carrying them in his bosom, / and leading the ewes with care.*

Responsorial Psalm 85: 9-10, 11-12, 13-14

2 Peter 3: 8-14 *The day of the Lord will come like a thief; he does not delay in keeping his promise. Rather, he shows you generous patience, since he wants none to perish but all to come to repentance. On that day the heavens will vanish with a roar; the elements will be destroyed by fire. While waiting for this, make every effort to be found without stain or defilement, and at peace in his sight.*

Mark 1: 1-8 *In Isaiah the prophet it is written: "I send my messenger before you to prepare your way; a herald's voice in the desert, crying, 'Make ready the way of the Lord.'" Thus John the Baptist appeared in the desert proclaiming a baptism of repentance which led to the forgiveness of sins. [John said:] "I have baptized you in water; he will baptize you in the Holy Spirit."*

Reflection:

Starting with today's chapter 40, the book of Isaiah contains the inspired thoughts of a different author, known as "Second Isaiah," who wants no recognition but to add, some 400 years later, to the message of the historical figure Isaiah the Prophet. His consoling message from Yahweh to his people points to an impending future release and return of the exiles from Babylon.

The promised Messiah will speak tenderly to poor beat-up Israel in Exile, assuring them that their time of punishment is over. God will now lead them back on a new, improved Interstate, with bridges over ravines, twists and turns made straight and safe, so that their Shepherd will gather them and carry them back, leading them with care. What a picture of a powerful God's gentle care for his wounded, worn-out flock.

In the opening verses of his gospel, Mark wastes no time in identifying John the Baptist with Isaiah's promised "voice in the desert" announcing the return home. Only now this new Exodus will lead, not home to the devastated Jerusalem they left behind, but home to the heavenly Jerusalem, where Jesus will go, to prepare a place for us with him in his risen glory!

The second letter of Peter presents a somber depiction of the end of the world. We prepare for the Day of the Lord by making every effort to remain devout in our conduct and at peace in his sight, all the way up to the day of his coming.

SECOND SUNDAY OF ADVENT
Cycle C – Scripture

Baruch 5:1-9 *Jerusalem, take off your robe of misery; put on the splendor of glory from God, for God will show all the earth your splendor: you will be named by God forever the peace of justice. Up, Jerusalem! Stand upon the heights; look to the east and see your children, rejoicing that they are remembered by God. Led away on foot by their enemies they left you: but God will bring them back to you borne aloft in glory as on royal thrones.*

Responsorial Psalm 126: 1-2, 2-3, 4-5, 6

Philippians 1:4-6, 8-11 *I am confident of this, that the one who began a good work in you will continue to complete it until the day of Christ Jesus. This is my prayer: that your love may increase ever more and more in knowledge and every kind of perception, to discern what is of value, so that you may be pure and blameless for the day of Christ.*

Luke 3:1-6 *In the fifteenth year of the reign of Tiberius Caesar, the word of God came to John the son of Zechariah in the desert. As it is written in the book of the prophet Isaiah: "A voice of one crying out in the desert: 'Prepare the way of the Lord, make straight his paths. Every valley shall be filled and every mountain and hill shall be made low. The winding roads shall be made straight, and the rough ways made smooth, and all flesh shall see the salvation of God.'"*

Reflection:

Baruch, who served as Jeremiah's secretary, writes during Jerusalem's lowest days, the time when her leading citizens, Temple leaders and the royal family were taken away into exile. God sends him to remind the people of the glory to come when He brings His people back, after they've learned their lesson, abandoning their sinful ways to once more walk hand-in-hand with God, because He will be true to the promised covenant, even if they weren't. Jerusalem will receive a new name (symbolizing a new start) and must exchange her miserable clothes for robes of glory. She must stand on the heights to see her children, once marched off as prisoners, now returning "borne aloft in glory as on royal thrones." Their progress will be made easy, as was the custom, by filling the valleys up and wearing the mountains down to make level their ground "that Israel may advance secure in the glory of God."

Luke fixes the arrival of Jesus firmly in the history of Jerusalem by introducing his precursor, John the Baptist, in great detail: 15th year of Tiberias Caesar, Pilate is the governor, Herod the tetrarch, when Annas and Caiaphas shared the high priesthood. John is the pinnacle of Old Testament preparation for the coming of the promised Messiah, quoting and fulfilling Isaiah's prophetic call for a voice in the desert to cry: "Prepare the way of the Lord, make straight his paths" lifting the valleys, lowering the hills, smoothing out the rough ways, so that "all flesh shall see the salvation of God."

It's interesting that this last phrase is not quoted in Mark's account (on which Luke based his own gospel) nor in Matthew's (which appeared before Luke's as well). Luke, the ex-Gentile, reminds us of the universality of God's salvation. His Messiah is sent not just to the people of the promise, but to all God's people, to the whole world. And so, it turns out, are we, when we are christened (anointed, Messiah'd) at our Baptism.

That is why Paul prays for us, in his letter to the Christians at Philippi, to grow more and more in the knowledge and discernment, purity and righteousness that comes to us through Christ for the glory and praise of God. Because he is sure that "the one who began a good work in you will continue to complete it until the day of Christ Jesus." There it is again, that final day, the <u>parousia</u>, when we come to full bloom in Christ as He comes to full stature in us, in His body the Church.

Monday Second Week

Scripture

Isaiah 35:1-10 *Strengthen the hands that are feeble, / make firm the knees that are weak, / Say to those whose hearts are frightened: / Be strong, fear not! / Here is your God, he comes to save you. / Then will the eyes of the blind be opened, / the ears of the deaf be cleared; / then will the lame leap like a stag, / then the tongue of the dumb will sing. / The burning sands will become pools, / and the thirsty ground, springs of water. / A highway will be there, / called the holy way; / and on it the redeemed will walk. / Those whom the LORD has ransomed will return / and enter Zion singing, / crowned with everlasting joy.*

Responsorial Psalm 85: 9-10, 11-12, 13-14

Luke 5:17-26 *One day as Jesus was teaching, the power of the Lord was with him for healing. And some men brought on a stretcher a man who was paralyzed; not finding a way to bring him in because of the crowd, they went up on the roof and lowered him on the stretcher through the tiles into the middle in front of Jesus. When he saw their faith, he said, "As for you, your sins are forgiven." Then the scribes and Pharisees began to ask themselves, "Who is this who speaks blasphemies? Who but God alone can forgive sins?" Jesus knew their thoughts and said to them in reply, "What are you thinking in your hearts? Which is easier, to say, 'Your sins are forgiven,' or to say, 'Rise and walk'? But that you may know that the Son of Man has*

authority on earth to forgive sins"--he said to the man who was para-
lyzed, "I say to you, rise, pick up your stretcher, and go home." He
stood up immediately before them, picked up what he had been lying
on, and went home, glorifying God. Then astonishment seized them
all and they glorified God, and, struck with awe, they said, "We have
seen incredible things today."

Reflection:

Isaiah paints a beautiful picture of the happy return home from
captivity, when God finally makes things right by redeeming his people.
The Jews will find that God has made the desert bloom for them, and
that burning sands have become, not mirages, but real pools of water,
that their way is now a highway, called the holy way! Those who walk
on it will meet no beast of prey, they'll be so safe they'll be singing
all the way home, and when they get there, God will crown them with
everlasting joy. God will remedy their physical (and, by extension,
their spiritual) ills, making feeble hands strong and weak knees firm.
He will open the eyes of the blind, clear the ears of the deaf, and the
mute will not just speak, but sing!

Jesus is God's instrument of healing; he begins the return to health
and peace and joy that God intends for those who live in his kingdom,
who return from their exile of sin to live with him in everlasting joy.
As Jesus is teaching, the roof above him is suddenly torn away and a
man on a litter is lowered before him. Jesus heals the man from what's
really ailing him, his sinful condition. But the murmuring provokes
him, so he spells it out for his critics. Either way, whether it's "Get
up!" or it's "Your sins are forgiven," God's healing power is clearly at
work. The body is the screen on which the movie plays—the healing
of the person, not just the body, is what God has promised and Jesus
is accomplishing.

Watch Jesus working, and you'll see the promised glory of the end-time
already beginning!

OUR LADY OF GUADALUPE, PATRONESS OF THE AMERICAS

Introduction:

When the young girl appears to St. Juan Diego and tells him "I am the mother of the true God, the creator, the Lord of the heavens and the earth," she does so not in Spanish (the language of the conquering Europeans) but in Nahuatl, his native tongue. Yet the image she leaves on his poncho, wonderfully preserved to this very day in the Basilica at the base of Tepeyac, shows her as Mexican, the result of the mix of Spaniards and natives. The rays of the sun shining behind her, and the moon beneath her feet, place both the masculine and feminine forces of nature at her service. Her tunic has the reddish-rose color of Huitzilo-pochtli, the Aztec supreme God of life. Her mantle is blue-green, the colors of heavenly divinity and of the fertile earth. Pregnant Aztec women would wear a sash loosely around the womb, with a little cross on it signifying the encounter between the ways of humanity and the ways of the divine. Mary's use of this symbol tells us she is pregnant with him who is the focal point of the encounter between God and humanity: Jesus. Through this miraculous image Mary announces the dawn of a new era of salvation for the New World.

Scripture

Zechariah 2:14-17 *Sing and rejoice, O daughter Zion! See, I am coming to dwell among you, says the LORD. Many nations shall join themselves to the LORD on that day, and they shall be his people, and he will dwell among you, and you shall know that the LORD of hosts has sent me to you. Silence, all mankind, in the presence of the LORD! For he stirs forth from his holy dwelling.*

Reflection:

Zechariah announces God's imminent arrival: "See, I am coming to dwell among you." In the prolog to John's Gospel (1:14) we read: "And the Word became flesh and made his dwelling among us," knowing that literally it means he pitched his tent among us—we remember the Jews were nomadic desert dwellers. In Luke's accounts, he takes up residence with/within us, in Mary's womb! No wonder daughter Zion is told to sing and rejoice!

There is an alternate first reading, from the Apocalypse of St. John, the Book of **Revelation 11:19a; 12: 1-6a, 10**. The woman in the vision depicted in chapter 12 matches surprisingly the one imaged on Juan Diego's poncho. The menacing dragon waiting to devour the child she is about to bear is thwarted by God's power, as "she gave birth to a son...destined to rule all the nations with an iron rod... [who is] caught up to God and his throne," while she is spirited away to safety in the desert. Are you thinking what I'm thinking? Daniel's apocalyptic vision (ch.7:13-14) of "one like a son of man coming on the clouds of heaven; when he reached the Ancient One and was presented before him, he received dominion, glory, and kingship...an everlasting dominion that shall not be taken away."

Responsorial Psalm 45: 11-12, 14-17

There are two choices for the **gospel** on this feast: **Luke 1:26-38**, the Annunciation, when Mary hears and responds to God's offer of motherhood, and **Luke 1:39-47**, the Visitation, when Mary receives her cousin Elizabeth's accolades and deflects them swiftly and humbly to the Lord. They appear as the gospels for December 20th and 21st, so please consult pp. 44 & 45 for text and reflection.

TUESDAY SECOND WEEK

Scripture

Isaiah 40: 1-11 (text p. 17, reflection p. 18)

Responsorial Psalm 96: 1-2, 3, 10, 11-12, 13

Matthew 18: 12-14 *Jesus said to his disciples: "A man owns a hundred sheep and one of them wanders away; will he not leave the ninety-nine and go in search of the stray? If he [finds] it, believe me he is happier about this one than about the ninety-nine that did not wander away. Just so, it is no part of your heavenly Father's plan that a single one of these little ones shall ever come to grief."*

Reflection:

A lovely parallel to Isaiah's Shepherd King who does not lord it over his charges, but goes after them in a search-and-rescue mission. We should not be surprised to learn that in the early church, their favorite depiction of Christ was the figure of the Good Shepherd, with a lamb tenderly and lovingly borne on his shoulders.

WEDNESDAY SECOND WEEK

Scripture

Isaiah 40:25-31 *Why, O Jacob, do you say, / "My way is hidden from the LORD, / and my right is disregarded by my God"?/ The LORD is the eternal God. / He does not faint nor grow weary. / They that hope in the LORD will renew their strength, / they will soar as with eagles' wings; / they will run and not grow weary, / walk and not grow faint.*

Responsorial Psalm 103: 1-2, 3-4, 8, 10

Matthew 11:28-30 *Take my yoke upon you and learn from me, for I am meek and humble of heart; and you will find rest for yourselves. For my yoke is easy, and my burden light.*

Reflection:

Isaiah's God addresses his people in their weariness. How can you question my awareness of your situation? I'm aware of every little detail in all of creation; I'm the reason everything holds together. But you complain that I have no regard for you? That I've lost track of you? On the contrary, it's you who have lost track of me; you've grown weary of my laws and my ways…. But remember: "They that hope in the Lord will renew their strength, they will soar as with eagles' wings; they will run and not grow weary, walk and not grow faint."

Jesus, the compassion of the Father, also has comforting words for the weary. In his concern for each of us, like the older brother that he is, he walks beside our every step, ready to share our burden. The image of the yoke is very telling, coming from a carpenter. Oxen were for the farmers of his day what a tractor is for us—they enabled a man to perform much heavier work than he could by himself. Great care was taken when a yoke was fitted for the oxen. If the carpenter did not measure it carefully and properly fit it to the contours of the animal's shoulders, it would chafe and weaken and injure the animal, instead of allowing its strength to be harnessed.

Picture yourself carrying a load that God has carefully and lovingly fitted to your capacities—you know He won't ask to do more than you can, especially if you turn and find Jesus alongside, helping you pull the load. His yoke, the yoke we share with him, is never too heavy nor too difficult, because we are not alone in our struggles. And, as he shares with us, can we not share with each other? Don't we know from experience that a sorrow shared is divided, whereas a joy shared is multiplied?

THURSDAY SECOND WEEK

Scripture

Isaiah 41:13-20 *Fear not, O worm Jacob, O maggot Israel; / I will make of you a threshing sledge, / sharp, new, and double-edged, / to thresh the mountains and crush them, / to make the hills like chaff. / I will turn the desert into a marshland, and the dry ground into springs of water. / That all may see and understand, / that the hand of the LORD has done this.*

Responsorial Psalm 145: 1, 9, 10-11, 12-13

Matthew 11:11-15 *He [John] is Elijah, the one who is to come. Whoever has ears ought to hear.*

Reflection:

Second Isaiah is the name given to the inspired but unknown author of chapters 40-55, who lived in Exile in Babylon, as opposed to the known prophet Isaiah, who was pre-Exilic. [The third section of the book, chapters 56-66, was the work of even later anonymous inspired writer(s) living back in Palestine after the people's return.]   He promises the people a wondrous reversal of fortune: from a lowly worm, a maggot, they will become the sharp metal teeth of a threshing sledge that can crush mountains, and from a parched desert springs of water!

And all this God will do so "that all may see…and understand…that the Holy One of Israel has [re]created it." "I, the Lord, will answer them; I, the God of Israel, will not forsake them." Even when we deservedly suffer for wandering away from God's love and companionship, his mercy comes to our rescue in answer to our prayer.

In the Gospel, Jesus identifies John the Baptist, his precursor, with the prophet Elijah, who will come before the world ends to announce the final victory of God's anointed, the Messiah. Thus Jesus clearly identifies himself as the Christ, the Messiah, the total embodiment of God's love and mercy coming to save us. Think of the em-body-ment that is taking shape in Mary's womb as we watch for her to give birth at Christmas.

FRIDAY SECOND WEEK

Scripture

Isaiah 48:17-19 *I, the LORD, your God, / lead you on the way you should go. / If you would hearken to my commandments, / your prosperity would be like a river, / your descendants would be like the sand, / their name never cut off / or blotted out from my presence.*

Responsorial Psalm 1: 1-2, 3, 4, 6

Matthew 11:16-19 *John came neither eating nor drinking, and they said, "He is possessed by a demon." The Son of Man came eating and drinking and they said, "Look, he is a glutton and a drunkard, a friend of tax collectors and sinners."*

Reflection:
The people suffer in Exile. They mourn the loss of God's favor, of their freedom, of their Temple—the visible sign of God's closeness to them. Yet Second Isaiah announces this consoling promise: "I, the Lord your God, lead you on the way you should go. If you would hearken to my commandments, your prosperity would be like a river." And their descendants would never again be removed from his presence.

Today's responsorial psalm praises the one who shuns the way of sinners, to follow God's lead "on the way you should go." The theme of living water, so precious to desert dwellers, reappears: "He is like a tree planted near running water...whose leaves never fade."

But the way on which God calls us is not always what we would expect. Jesus chides the crowds for complaining that his cousin John was a wacko because he would avoid their eating and drinking to devote himself to asceticism, disciplining himself so as to make room for the coming Messiah in his life. And then the same people complain against Jesus that he is a glutton and a drunkard because he sits down to eat with sinners when he reaches out to invite them into the true banquet of life from which his Abba will not exclude them. Are we paying less attention to ourselves so we can pay more attention to Christ's call? Do our hearts harbor little lists of people we refuse to include, when we know our Messianic vocation is to reach out to "outsiders"?

SATURDAY SECOND WEEK

Scripture

Sirach 48:1-4, 9-11 *How awesome are you, ELIJAH! You were taken aloft in a whirlwind, in a chariot with fiery horses. You are destined to come before the day of the LORD, and to reestablish the tribes of Jacob.*

Responsorial Psalm 80: 2-3, 15-16, 18-19

Matthew 17:10-13 *"Elijah will indeed come and restore all things; but I tell you that Elijah has already come, and they did not recognize him but did to him whatever they pleased. So also will the Son of Man suffer at their hands."*

Reflection:
Today's Eucharist has rightly been called "the Elijah Mass." This All-Star prophet lived in the 8th century B.C. His death is not record-ed; instead he vanishes "in the whirlwind" in a fiery chariot (2Kings

2:11) and God promises through the prophet Malachi (3:23) "I am going to send you Elijah the prophet before my day comes, that great and terrible day," so that it's the obvious warning of the end of time for God's people.

With the appearance of John the Baptist preaching a renewed preparation for God's coming, listeners are reminded of Elijah's role. Even the responsorial psalm speaks in terms of the final days: "Rouse your power and come to save us…take care of this vine, and protect what your right hand has planted…then we will no more withdraw from you." (The vine planted, rejected, and restored is a favorite Old Testament figure for God's people and their situation in his care.)

Jesus makes clear in his answer to his disciples that Elijah, whose coming "will restore everything," has already come. That is, the warning that the Messiah is at hand to renew God's closeness to his people, has already been delivered by John the Baptist, who went not only unrecognized and unappreciated, but was put to death for his troubles. Jesus takes the occasion to prepare his friends: "The Son of Man will suffer at their hands in the same way." Are we making ready for God's coming close to us? How?

THIRD SUNDAY OF ADVENT

Like a good, understanding mother, the Church knows when to offer encouragement in the midst of prolonged efforts. On this third of the four Sundays of Advent, she puts on rose-colored vestments, and labels it "Gaudete Sunday," from St. Paul's opening line today: "Rejoice! Again I say to you, rejoice!" [We'll see this again in the even more protracted series of Lenten Sundays, when the fourth of the six Sundays uses rose for vestments in the midst of penitential purple, and the consoling verse is "Laetare!" "Be glad!" Notice it's toned down from the Rejoice! of Advent, but it still offers a breather.]

Cycle A – Scripture

Isaiah 35: 1-6, 10 *The desert and the parched land will exult; / they will bloom with abundant flowers. / They will see the glory of the Lord. / Strengthen the hands that are feeble, / make firm the knees that are week, / say to those whose hearts are frightened: / Be strong, fear not! / Here is your God, he comes to save you. / Then will the eyes of the blind be opened, / the ears of the deaf be cleared. / Then will the lame leap like a stag, / then the tongue of the dumb will sing. / Those whom the Lord has ransomed will return / and enter Zion singing, / crowned with everlasting joy.*

Responsorial Psalm 146: 6-7, 8-9, 9-10

James 5: 7-10 *Be patient, my brothers, until the coming of the Lord. As your models in suffering hardships and in patience, take the prophets who spoke in the name of the Lord.*

Matthew 11: 2-11 From prison, John the Baptist sent his disciples to ask Jesus if he was the one, or should they be waiting for another. Jesus tells them to report to John what he's been doing: *"the blind recover their sight, cripples walk, lepers are cured, the deaf hear, dead men are raised to life, and the poor have the good news preached to them."*

Reflection:

Isaiah depicts the glorious return from exile with the whole desert breaking into bloom. Even the exiled are blooming: no more feeble hands or weak knees or frightened hearts. In fact, God will remove their afflictions: deaf ears will hear, blind eyes will see, mute tongues will sing! Matthew reports this exact happening in the ministry of Jesus, clearly assigning him the long-awaited Messianic role.

And the Apostle James teaches an Advent lesson when he exhorts us to be patient, confidently expecting the arrival of God's promised one.

THIRD SUNDAY OF ADVENT

Cycle B – Scripture

Isaiah 61: 1-2, 10-11 *The spirit of the Lord is upon me, / because the Lord has anointed me; / he has sent me to bring glad tidings to the lowly, / to heal the brokenhearted, / to proclaim liberty to captives / and release to prisoners, / to announce a year of favor from the Lord / and a day of vindication by our God.*

Responsorial Psalm – Luke 1:46-48, 49-50, 53-54
1 Thessalonians 5:16-24 *Rejoice always, never cease praying, render constant thanks, such is God's will for you in Christ Jesus. May you be preserved irreproachable at the coming of our Lord Jesus Christ.*

John 1: 6-8, 19-28 John introduces the Baptist as one sent by God to testify on behalf of Jesus.

Reflection:
The Jews believed that the prophet Elijah, who never died but was taken up in a fiery chariot, would return in Messianic times and announce the end of the world. From the angel's announcement to Zechariah, little John is explicitly connected with Jesus as the Elijah who would recognize and testify on behalf of Jesus' Messianic mission, introducing the Day of the Lord. Never does the Baptist claim any position or credit for himself; he always points to the one coming after him, the one God will send to get the job done.

THIRD SUNDAY OF ADVENT
Cycle C – Scripture

Zephaniah 3:14-18 *The LORD, your God, will rejoice over you with gladness; he will sing joyfully because of you, as one sings at festivals.*

Responsorial Psalm – Isaiah 12: 2-3, 4, 5-6

Philippians 4:4-7 *Rejoice in the Lord always. I shall say it again: rejoice! The peace of God that surpasses all understanding will guard your hearts and minds in Christ Jesus.*

Luke 3:10-18 *And the crowds asked him, "What then should we do?" He said, "Whoever has two cloaks should share with the person who has none. And whoever has food should do likewise." Even tax collectors came to be baptized and they said, "Teacher, what should we do?" He answered, "Stop collecting more than what is prescribed." Soldiers also asked him, "And what is it that we should do?" He told them, "Do not practice extortion, do not falsely accuse anyone, and be satisfied with your wages." Now the people were filled with expectation, and all were asking in their hearts whether John might be the Messiah.*

Reflection:

Zephaniah presents an unusual image of our God singing for joy—over us! We're so often reminded ("for our own good?") of our sinfulness, yet here comes a God who is so happy to see us that he breaks into song! How's that for building up our self-esteem? God is in our midst, a mighty Savior who will renew us in his love; we have nothing to fear. Advent in a capsule: our joy is based on God's joy, coming right at us, bringing us a peace that's beyond our imagining, so much more than just the absence of war, a peace born of God's intimacy with us, enveloping us.

St. Luke's gospel gives us a unique report on the preaching of John the Baptist to his varied and interesting audience: the (Jewish) crowds get wonderfully practical advice about sharing; "even tax collectors," collaborators with the occupying forces and thus generally shunned by all "good" Jews, receive clear and concise advice; and then soldiers (who'd have thought these foreigners assigned to subjugate the Jews to Rome would be open to or even seeking spiritual pointers from a Jewish prophet out in the desert?) are told how to improve their daily lives. No wonder people start to wonder if John might not be the Messiah sent to prepare them for God's arrival.

But the best part of the good news of God's coming is how he makes his presence known. If it were explicit, so that we couldn't help but actually see him, the very force of his presence would compel our behavior. If he comes in the everyday unexceptional events of our lives (cf. John's advice) then we can actually choose to sense his loving presence in ourselves and each other, to recognize it, to aid and abet it by our simple deferrals to his unseen but felt presence. Force compels— only love can invite a loving response. Our God comes in love, he is love. We can hardly wait....

N.B. The Octave of Christmas, from December 17 on, has its proper Mass for each day. So beginning on the 17th please move on to "Stage Two of Advent" p. 39.
Meanwhile, back at the ranch...

MONDAY THIRD WEEK

Scripture

Numbers 24: 2-7, 15-17 Balaam, a famous wise man from the East, is summoned to cast a spell on the advancing Israelites in the Plains of Moab, in the 13th century B.C. Instead, after *"the spirit of God came* *upon him,"* he'll predict a glorious future king for this people. *"I see him, though not now; I behold him, though not near. A star shall advance from Jacob, and a staff shall rise from Israel."*

Responsorial Psalm 25: 4-5, 6-7, 8-9

Matthew 21: 23-27 When the chief priests and elders of the people demand that Jesus tell them on what authority he acts, he counters: First you tell me, what was the origin of John's baptism—divine or human? They thought if they answered "divine" Jesus could ask them why they didn't put faith in him; but if they said "human" they would offend the people, who considered John a prophet. So they said "We don't know." Jesus retorted "Then neither will I tell you on what authority I do the things I do."

Reflection:
The first reading sets the scene for the Three Wise Men from the East who appear in Matthew's account of the birth of Jesus. Baalam is asked to cast a spell against the Israelites who threaten Moab, but instead is moved to predict the coming of a mighty king, whose arrival will be signaled by a star! The Magi will appear in Jerusalem following a star that will bring them to the Newborn King.

In the gospel Jesus puts the attacking authorities on the defensive by a simple counter-proposal. If they will take a stand on the Baptist, his precursor, then he will answer their question. They can't, of course, without losing face, because they knew in their hearts that John's message was from God—they just weren't ready to accept it. But they won't acknowledge it, so Jesus plays coy with them too.

TUESDAY THIRD WEEK

Scripture

Zephaniah 3: 1-2, 9-13 *Woe to the city, rebellious and polluted! / She accepts no correction; / in the Lord she has not trusted. / But I will leave as a remnant in your midst / a people humble and lowly, / who shall take refuge in the name of the Lord. / They shall pasture their flocks / with none to disturb them.*

Responsorial Psalm 34: 2-3, 6-7, 17-18, 19, 23

Matthew 21: 28-32 Jesus addresses a parable to the chief priests and elders of the people, about a man who asks, in turn, his two sons to go work at their vineyard. The first is quick to answer, Yes sir! But he's all talk, he never does go out. The second said, Nope, I'm busy, but later thinks better of it and goes to work. Jesus pointedly asks for their opinion: Which of the two did what the father wanted? The second, they answered. Then Jesus goes on the attack mode: Haven't I been telling you that tax collectors and prostitutes will be entering the king-dom of heaven ahead of you? When John the Baptist came, preaching a way of holiness, you put no faith in him, but they did!

Reflection:

Zephaniah predicts a terrible "Day of the Lord" for the unruly citizens of Jerusalem, so that they learn their lesson the hard way. But he speaks of a remnant (the anawim) who remain faithful and submissive to God, and thus enjoy his favor. In the Gospel we find Jesus desperately trying to alert the leaders to the danger of their intransigence. They would do well to emulate those public sinners they shun, in their openness to the saving message of God's offered kingdom now upon them.

WEDNESDAY THIRD WEEK

Scripture

Isaiah 45: 6-8, 18, 21-25 *I am the Lord, there is no other. / Turn to me and be safe, / all you ends of the earth. / In the Lord shall be the vindication and the glory / of all the descendants of Israel.*
Responsorial Psalm 85: 9-10, 11-12, 13-14

Luke 7: 18-23 *John sent [two of his disciples] to ask the Lord, "Are you 'He who is to come' or are we to expect someone else?" Jesus [responded], "Go and report to John what you have seen and heard. The blind recover their sight, cripples walk, lepers are cured, the deaf hear, dead men are raised to life, and the poor have the good news preached to them."*

Reflection:

For Isaiah the Messianic times will bring the vindication of the chosen people: all their suffering will be removed, and all their glory restored. Not only they, but the whole world will turn to the Messiah and find safety. Luke shows Jesus in action as the outreach, the active agent for God's justice and healing of all our ills.

THURSDAY THIRD WEEK

Scripture

Isaiah 54: 1-10 Be happy, you once-barren who bore no children, because your descendants will one day populate cities that are now desolate. Worry no more about being widowed, because your new husband is your Maker, and your redeemer is the Holy One of Israel. *"For a brief moment I abandoned you, but with great tenderness I will* *take you back."* The Lord has mercy on you, and promises that his love will never again leave you.

Responsorial Psalm 30: 2, 4, 5-6, 11-12, 13

Luke 7: 24-30 *When the messengers of John had set off, Jesus began to speak of him to the crowds. "This is the man of whom Scripture says, 'I send my messenger ahead of you to prepare your way before you.' I assure you, there is no man born of woman greater than John. Yet the least born into the kingdom of God is greater than he."*

Reflection:

Isaiah reassures the people that their God was just trying to teach them a lesson—he would never abandon them and call it quits. His love is too great to be stopped by our unfaithfulness, so he will continue to show us (unmerited) mercy. And in the Gospel, Jesus will lavish praise on his cousin John, but add clearly that coming into God's kingdom with him will place us even closer to holiness. John had his job to do, preparing for the Messiah to be recognized and heard by the people, but our Baptismal Messianic task is even greater: to bring others into the reign of God.

FRIDAY THIRD WEEK

Scripture

Isaiah 56: 1-3, 6-8 *Let not the foreigner say, / when he wanted to join himself to the Lord, / "The Lord will surely exclude me from his people." / All who keep the Sabbath from profanation / and hold to my covenant / I will bring to my holy mountain. / For my house shall be called / a house of prayer for all peoples. / Thus says the Lord God.*

Responsorial Psalm 67: 2-3, 5, 7-8

John 5: 33-36 *Jesus said to the Jews: "You have sent to John, who has testified to the truth. Yet I have a testimony greater than John's, namely, the works the Father has given me to accomplish. These very works which I perform testify on my behalf that the Father has sent me."*

Reflection:

When the exiles returned from Babylon (536 B.C.) they were encouraged to be truly religious and not turn away any interested Gentiles. Isaiah emphasizes how God wants his house to be for <u>all peoples</u>. And Jesus accepts the testimony of John, but moves out beyond the O.T. and sets up his agenda of performing the works his Father asks him to carry out. These are also clearly universal, because he reaches out to sinners, rejects, and Gentiles alike, bringing them all the invitation from his Father and theirs to come into the reign of God, and to become part of a holier, all-encompassing family.

INTRODUCTION TO STAGE TWO OF ADVENT

This stage consists of the octave before Christmas, when our watching/preparing is intensified. (These designated Masses give way only to the 3rd/4th Sunday of Advent.) The Church prescribes the use of the second of its two Advent Prefaces, featuring the Old Testament prophets, John the Baptist and the Virgin Mary herself to call our attention to Christ's approaching arrival.

As regards our readings, the eight most famous Messianic predictions make up the O.T. portion. The Gospels are selections from the so-called "Infancy Narratives" which begin the life of Jesus in Matthew and Luke, each making a bridge from the promise of the Old Testament to its fulfillment in the coming of Jesus in the New. Matthew's traditional, patriarchal approach hinges on Joseph as receiver of angelic messages, while Luke (non-Jewish) uses Mary as the focus of events leading up to Jesus' birth.

Between the 17th and the 23rd the liturgy assigns the famous "O Antiphons," short prayers rich in references to the Scriptures and packed with O.T. expectations of the Messiah. As we read on p. 131 of the <u>Vatican II Weekday Missal</u>: "The unknown author of these beautiful prayers lived around the 6th or 7th Christian century [and] chose seven titles whose first letters are S-A-R-C-O-R-E." The titles for Christ are: O Sapientia (wisdom), O Adonai (Hebrew for Lord), O Radix Jesse (root of Jesse), O Clavis David (key of David), O Oriens (rising sun), O Rex (king), and O Emmanuel (God-with-us). When read backwards, the acronym renders the Latin <u>ero cras</u>: Tomorrow I will be. Neat, huh? [These "Great Antiphons" serve as the Alleluia verses introducing the Gospel selections.]

December 17th – Scripture

Genesis 49: 2, 8-10 *Jacob called his sons and said to them: "Assemble and listen, sons of Jacob. You, Judah, shall your brothers praise, the sons of your father shall bow down to you. The scepter shall never depart from Judah."*

Responsorial Psalm 72: 3-4, 7-8, 17

Matthew 1: 1-17 Matthew opens his Gospel with the genealogy of Jesus Christ, son of David, son of Abraham. He traces downward from Abraham to Joseph, the husband of Mary, in a contrived trio of 14-generation groups, covering the patriarchs, the royal family, and the "nobodies" who appeared after the return from Babylon.

Reflection:
We go all the way back to the 18th century B.C. and hear Jacob predict the future for each of his twelve sons' families (the 12 tribes of Israel, a synonym for Jacob). Jacob predicts supremacy for the tribe of Judah. King David (and the King of Kings) will issue from this tribe. And from the opening words of his gospel, Matthew will introduce Jesus

Christ (that is, Jesus the Messiah) as son of David—their Hero-King par excellence, and son of Abraham—the source and father of all things Jewish. Make no mistake about it: Jesus is the one God planned to send to rescue us.

December 18th – Scripture

Jeremiah 23:5-8 *I will raise up a righteous shoot to David; as king he shall reign and govern wisely.*

Responsorial Psalm 72:1, 12-13, 18-19

Matthew 1:18-24 *When his mother Mary was betrothed to Joseph, but before they lived together, she was found with child through the holy Spirit. Joseph, her husband, decided to divorce her quietly when, behold, the angel of the Lord appeared to him in a dream and said, "Joseph, son of David, do not be afraid to take Mary your wife into your home. For it is through the holy Spirit that this child has been conceived in her." When Joseph awoke, he did as the angel of the Lord had commanded him and took his wife into his home.*

Reflection:
Jeremiah's prophesy gives hope for the future, even as the Southern Kingdom (Judah) is collapsing under Babylonian attack. A new king will come, after they return from the North (across the desert—again— a new Exodus). And then "they shall again live on their own land," because this new king "shall do what is just and right in the land."

The responsorial psalm elucidates: "He shall rescue the poor man when he cries out, and the afflicted when he has no one to help him [the people in Exile]. He shall have pity for the lowly and the poor; the lives of the poor he shall save." This will be their situation when the people return from Babylon to their ruined homeland: no Temple, no palaces, no prosperity, no prospects, seemingly. But "blessed be the

Lord, the God of Israel, who alone does wondrous deeds." It will take wonders to return the beaten-down people to normalcy, but God assures them of his mercy.

The awaited Messiah will accomplish this reversal, when he comes to set things right. And Matthew's gospel situates Jesus as the promised Christ (Messiah) as he tells of Joseph acting as Jesus' legal father and adopting him into the royal Davidic line. This is more important than it might seem at first glance: Jesus the son of Mary has no legal standing in Jewish patriarchal society; Jesus the son of Joseph as Mary's husband belongs to the royal family's promised never-ending kingship. God works wonders for his little ones, as Mary will soon joyfully sing.

December 19th – Scripture

Judges 13:2-7, 24-25 *There was a certain man, whose name was Manoah. His wife was barren. An angel of the LORD appeared to the woman and said, "Though you are barren and have had no children, yet you will conceive and bear a son. Take no wine or strong drink and eat nothing unclean. As for your son, no razor shall touch his head, for this boy is to be consecrated to God from the womb. He will begin the deliverance of Israel from the power of the Philistines." The woman bore a son and named him Samson, and the LORD blessed him.*

Responsorial Psalm 71: 3-4, 5-6, 16-17

Luke 1:5-25 *There was a priest named Zechariah; his wife was from the daughters of Aaron, and her name was Elizabeth. The angel said to him, "Do not be afraid, Zechariah, because your prayer has been heard. Your wife Elizabeth will bear you a son, and you shall name him John. He will be filled with the holy Spirit even from his mother's womb, and he will turn many of the children of Israel to the Lord their God. He will go before him in the spirit and power of Elijah to prepare a people fit for the Lord."*

Reflection:

We are prepared for the upcoming announcement of Jesus' birth
by today's twin events: from deep in Israel's history the promise of
Samson's arrival, and from the very threshold of the New Testament
the promise of John the Baptist's coming. The Book of Judges covers
the historical period between Joshua's entry into what would become
their new homeland, and the first of the kings, Saul, who would rule
the people in God's stead. As the Israelites encountered local persecu-
tion and opposition, God would raise leaders, known collectively as
"Judges," to rescue his people from their plight.

An angel announces to the nameless, and heretofore childless, wife of
Manoah that she will have a son "consecrated to God from the womb
until the day of his death." Samson will be under the "Nazirite vow,"
the visible response to God's choice by never having his hair cut. "He
grew up and the Lord blessed him. The Spirit of the Lord began to be
with him." He rose up to resist the Philistines, and, as they say, the rest
is, (thanks to Delilah, delightful) history.

By Jesus' time, the descendants of Aaron's priestly tribe were so
numerous that they were subdivided into classes, which would be
called seasonally to serve at the Temple. When Zechariah, husband
of Mary's cousin Elizabeth, is chosen from his class to enter into the
sanctuary, he receives the unlikely news of impending fatherhood.
Again, the child will be "filled with the Holy Spirit from his mother's
womb." This time the Nazirite vow extends the prohibition of wine
or strong drink to the child, besides no cutting of hair. And isn't it
interesting that the angel already identifies little John with Elijah?

December 20th – Scripture

Isaiah 7:10-14 *The LORD spoke to Ahaz: Ask for a sign from the
LORD. But Ahaz answered, "I will not ask! I will not tempt the
LORD!" Then he said: Listen, the Lord himself will give you this*

sign: the virgin shall be with child, and bear a son, and shall name him Emmanuel.

Responsorial Psalm 24: 1-2, 3-4, 5-6

Luke 1:26-38 *In the sixth month, the angel Gabriel was sent from God to a virgin betrothed to a man named Joseph. Coming to her, he said, "Hail, favored one! The Lord is with you. You have found favor with God. Behold, you will conceive in your womb and bear a son, and you shall name him Jesus." Mary said to the angel, "How can this be, since I have no relations with a man?" And the angel said, "The holy Spirit will come upon you, and the power of the Most High will over-shadow you." Mary said, "Behold, I am the handmaid of the Lord. May it be done to me according to your word."*

Reflection:

In the good old days of Latin, this was called the Missa Aurea, the "Golden Mass" since it marked the first step in Jesus' arrival in our midst—he takes up residence in the womb of his Virgin Mother. Isaiah reports God's frustration at the outwardly submissive King Ahaz, whose reluctance to ask for a sign ("I will not tempt the Lord") masks the fact that he has already, on his own, sought protection for his kingdom from an alliance with other (pagan) kings. Can you imagine: ruling in Yahweh's name and not trusting in God to come to his aid but instead turning to pagans for help?

So Isaiah relays God's glorious promised sign: "the virgin [in Hebrew almah, a young girl and therefore virginal] shall…bear a son, and shall name him Emmanuel," which means God-is-with-us. In the later, Spirit-filled understanding of the Apostles, Mary's virginity was not seen as an automatic reflection of her youth, but as reflecting her conscious choice to remain totally faithful to God's wonderful call to the motherhood of his Son. (What the Church would render in the Latin virgo rather than the Hebrew almah.)

Mary's question to the angel contains none of the intransigence of Ahaz's objection to Isaiah. She simply wonders how God will bring about her pregnancy, since she has no man in her future. Learning that God will take care of this himself, through the power of the Holy Spirit, she graciously submits to his plan. Ta-da! Let the adventure begin!

December 21st – Scripture

Song of Songs 2:8-14 *My lover speaks, he says to me: Arise, my beloved, my beautiful one, and come! Let me see you; let me hear your voice; for your voice is sweet, and you are lovely.*

Luke 1:39-45 *Mary set out and traveled to the hill country in haste to a town of Judah, where she entered the house of Zechariah and greeted Elizabeth. When Elizabeth heard Mary's greeting, the infant leaped in her womb, and Elizabeth, filled with the holy Spirit, cried out in a loud voice and said, "Most blessed are you among women, and blessed is the fruit of your womb. For at the moment the sound of your greeting reached my ears, the infant in my womb leaped for joy. Blessed are you who believed that what was spoken to you by the Lord would be fulfilled."*

Reflection:
The Song of Songs is attributed to King Solomon, and tells in poetic fashion the story of the love between God and his people as demonstrated by the love of the young woman who speaks in today's selection and her bridegroom, rushing over the hills to visit her. The image of a gazelle leaping joyfully and effortlessly on all fours (boing!boing!boing!) springs to mind (get it?) from the TV nature reporting we've all seen, and leaves a vivid impression. How exciting for the young lovers! He peers through the lattice and calls softy but urgently to her: "Arise, come out, let me see you, let me hear your sweet voice." All this love is from God. All this love is in God. And we are the targets of his love!

[The **alternate** first reading **Zephaniah 3:14-18** has been discussed in the commentary on the readings of the 3rd Sunday of Advent, p. 33.]

Luke tells the story of the Visitation of Elizabeth by her cousin Mary. After the angel told her Elizabeth was in her sixth month, Mary hurries over to spend the next (guess how many…that's right:) three months with her. After all, her cousin is an older woman expecting her first child, and Mary is a young, able-bodied and loving relative who can pitch in nicely…. It was around a seventy-mile journey, so it probably took close to a week to get there, but as soon as she greets her cousin, Mary begins to see the wonders of God's love at work. The little cousins have the world's first womb-to-womb not-quite-cordless communication! And Elizabeth, filled with the Holy Spirit, sings the praises of her young cousin, "who [also] trusted that the Lord's words to her would be fulfilled." And soon they will be…yipee!

December 22nd – Scripture

First Samuel 1:24-28 *"Pardon, my lord! As you live my lord, I am the woman who stood near you here, praying to the LORD. I prayed for this child, and the LORD granted my request. Now I, in turn, give him to the LORD; as long as he lives, he shall be dedicated to the LORD." She left him there.*

Responsorial Psalm – 1 Samuel 2: 1, 4-5, 6-7, 8

Luke 1:46-56 *And Mary said: "My soul proclaims the greatness of the Lord; my spirit rejoices in God my savior. For he has looked upon his handmaid's lowliness; behold, from now on will all ages call me blessed. The Mighty One has done great things for me, and holy is his name. He has helped Israel his servant, remembering his mercy, according to his promise to our fathers, to Abraham and to his descendants forever."*

Reflection:

In the first Book of Samuel, chapter one, we read the story of Elkanah and his (second) wife Hannah. He preferred her to his other wife, who had given him many children, but, alas! Hannah remained childless. "Her rival would taunt her to annoy her…this went on year after year." On one visit to the Temple at Shiloh, she prayed to Yahweh that if he would just give her a son, she would "give him to Yahweh for the whole of his life and no razor [would] ever touch his head."

I love this part: "While she prayed before Yahweh, which she did for some time, Eli [the priest there] was watching her mouth, for she was speaking under her breath; her lips were moving but her voice could not be heard. He therefore supposed that she was drunk," and proceeded to berate her. When she explained her great sorrow he asked God to grant her request. Little Samuel was born, to her great joy, and as soon as she weaned him…(now on to today's reading). Is God good, or what?

The first ten verses of chapter two of the book contain Hannah's grateful response—a hymn of praise to God. Please don't miss it; parts are quoted for today's responsorial psalm. Mary's own song of praise, deferring Elizabeth's congratulations of herself over to God, is clearly an echo of Hannah's song, which in my good old Jerusalem Bible includes over thirty references/footnotes, as she revisits the entire Old Testament in celebrating God's constant care for his little ones. It should not surprise us how well young Mary knew her Bible; what a lovely preparation she must have received in the saintly home of Joachim and Anne.

December 23rd – Scripture

Malachi 3:1-4, 23-24 *Yes, he is coming, says the LORD of hosts. But who will endure the day of his coming? For he is like the refiner's fire, and he will purify the sons of Levi, refining them like gold or like silver. Then the sacrifice of Judah and Jerusalem will please the LORD, as in* *days of old, as in years gone by. Lo, I will send you Elijah, the prophet, before the day of the LORD comes, the great and terrible day.*

Responsorial Psalm 25: 4-5, 8-9, 10, 14

Luke 1:57-66 *Elizabeth gave birth to a son. Her neighbors and relatives rejoiced with her. When they came on the eighth day to circumcise the child, they were going to call him Zechariah after his father, but his mother said in reply, "No. He will be called John." But they answered her, "There is no one among your relatives who has this name." So they made signs, asking his father what he wished him to be called. He asked for a tablet and wrote, "John is his name," and all were amazed. Immediately his mouth was opened, his tongue freed, and he spoke blessing God. All who heard these things took them to heart, saying, "What, then, will this child be?" For surely the hand of the Lord was with him.*

Reflection:

Malachi was prompted to chastise the priests of his time, predicting that God would send Elijah to cleanse the Temple and rectify matters before the Messiah's arrival. "Lo, I will send you Elijah, the prophet, before the day of the Lord comes, the great and terrible day." Things have gotten so bad that the sons of Levi (the priests) must be refined like gold in a fire, so that their sacrifices will once again "please the Lord, as in the days of old, as in years gone by."

Luke tells the story of the birth of John the Baptist, who, after the five centuries since Malachi, is the next prophet sent by God to his people. His miraculous appearance (aged parents, Zechariah's vision and regained speech) reawakens the people's wonderment, and raises expectations of his role in God's coming closer to us again. All this takes place at his circumcision, when he is to receive his father's name, of course. When Elizabeth demurs, they ask Zechariah about it, "using signs." Don't you love it? He signaled for a writing tablet and wrote the words: "I'm mute, I'm not deaf, you can talk to me! And listen to his mother, 'cause his name is John." Bingo!

"At that moment his mouth was opened and his tongue loosed, and he began to speak in praise of God." What a story! How impressed they must have been with his tale of the appearance of the angel at the Temple sanctuary, "standing at the right of the altar of incense" (lovely detail, no?) Luke 1:11ff. In the tradition of men chosen by God for a special mission, he will be under the Naziritic vow, "he will drink neither wine nor strong drink" and "will be filled with the Holy Spirit from his mother's womb" and will act "in the spirit and power of Elijah." If this baby is the new Elijah, can the Messiah be far behind?

December 24th – Scripture

2 Samuel 7: 1-5, 8-12, 14, 16 When David realizes how blest he has been, delivered from all his enemies, safely enjoying a lovely palace, it doesn't seem right for Yahweh's dwelling place among us to be in a tabernacle (a tent). Nathan agrees it seems a good idea to build the ark a fancier protective structure. But later that night the Lord speaks clearly to Nathan: You tell that boy, he's going to build a house for me? I'm the one who's provided for him every step of the way. But he means well, so you tell him: *The Lord will establish a house for you. Your house and your kingdom shall endure forever before me; your throne shall stand firm forever."*

Responsorial Psalm 89:2-3, 4-5, 27, 29

Luke 1: 67-79 Zechariah, overwhelmed by God's favor in sending them young John, sends up a canticle of praise to God for his entire history of dealing mercifully with his people: his promise to the house of David, preceded by his covenants with Abraham and Moses. And finally, for the pivotal role his son John will play in the immediate preparation of the people for the arrival of their long-awaited Messiah, who will guide our feet into the way of peace.

Reflection:
From 2 Samuel we have the guarantee of God's unending rule over his people through the Davidic Monarchy, and from Luke we almost see the Messiah's foot on the threshold of history, with John the Baptist doing his best Ed McMahon intro (for a different J.C.), "Heeeeeere's Jesus!"

FOURTH SUNDAY OF ADVENT
Cycle A – Scripture

Isaiah 7: 10-14 *Listen, O house of David! The Lord himself will give you this sign: the virgin shall be with child, and bear a son, and shall name him Emmanuel.*

Responsorial Psalm 24: 1-2, 3-4, 5-6

Romans 1: 1-7 *[I, Paul] preach the gospel concerning the Son, who was descended from David according to the flesh but was made Son of God in power, according to the spirit of holiness, by his resurrection from the dead.*

Matthew 1: 18-24 *"Joseph, have no fear about taking Mary as your wife. It is by the Holy Spirit that she has conceived this child." All this happened to fulfill what the Lord had said through the prophet: "The virgin shall be with child and give birth to a son, and they shall call him Emmanuel," a name which means "God is with us."*

Reflection:
King Ahaz's fake show of humility exasperates Isaiah, who then simply blurts out the wonderful sign to come: the promise of a young girl

of the royal house who will bear a son so holy that he will be called God-is-with-us. In Paul we receive a description of Christ who is at the same time descended from David in the flesh, and also obviously the Son of God in the spirit of holiness, by virtue of the awesome power of his resurrection from the dead. The gospel is Matthew's chance to demonstrate the old Isaian prophecy's fulfillment in his own N.T. times.

FOURTH SUNDAY OF ADVENT
Cycle B – Scripture

2 Samuel 7: 1-5, 8-11, 16 [please see p. 49]

Responsorial Psalm 89: 2-3, 4-5, 27, 29

Romans 16: 25-27 *To him who strengthen[s] you in the gospel which reveals the mystery hidden for many ages but now manifested through the prophets, to him may glory be given through Jesus Christ.*

Luke 1: 26-38 [please see p. 44]

Reflection:
From roughly 1,000 B.C. we read Yahweh's grateful response to David's solicitude for a more decent place for housing his ark, anchoring his presence among his people. God promises to maintain David's "house," his lineage, his royal family, in perpetuity. When Jesus appears, in the very town of David, as his descendant, this prophecy finds its final focus. Our second reading also ties in with Advent expectation, because it shows the prophets' words bringing about the unveiling of the mystery of Christ who has finally appeared.

FOURTH SUNDAY OF ADVENT
Cycle C – Scripture

Micah 5:1-4 *Bethlehem-Ephrathah, too small to be among the clans of Judah, from you shall come forth for me one who is to be ruler in Israel; he shall stand firm and shepherd his flock by the strength of the LORD, in the majestic name of the LORD, his God; he shall be peace.*

Responsorial Psalm 80: 2-23, 15-16, 18-19

Hebrews 10: 5-10 *First he says, "Sacrifices and offerings, holocausts and sin offerings, you neither desired nor delighted in." These are offered according to the law. Then he says, "Behold, I come to do your will." He takes away the first to establish the second. By this "will," we have been consecrated through the offering of the body of Jesus Christ once for all.*

Reflection:

Micah's recognition of little Bethlehem's pivotal role follows the tradition of God's choice of "losers" to carry out his grand designs. David vs. Goliath is like Michael J. Fox with a slingshot in the back pocket of his jeans taking on Arnold Schwarzenegger in a suit of armor, but guess who wins? The fortified walls of Jericho give way not to Special Forces or Green Berets but to the drum and bugle corps. How much clearer can God make it for us that it's his power and not our strength that gains our victories?

"He shall shepherd his flock by the strength of the Lord, in the majestic name of the Lord, his God." So it turns out that in John's chapter 10, when Jesus announces "I am the good shepherd," he's really laying claim to the Messianic kingship that is his by virtue of his lineage from David, the shepherd-king who hails from Bethlehem. And consider the power of that final phrase: not, he shall bring peace, but, "he shall be peace."

Placed between the promise of a king of peace and the joy of the Visitation, this passage from the Letter to the Hebrews is a sobering reminder that the cross is never far from the crib. Our thoughts go from Christmas to Calvary, because we know Jesus took on our human existence so that he could lift it from slavery to sin into the freedom of God's own life. The author was particularly interested in Temple rituals and the value of sacrificial offerings in gaining us God's favor. The old offerings were seen as cleansing and consecrating the people to God. Jesus' sacrificial death does so "once for all," no need for any more ritual killing of animals ever again, since Christ destroys the power of sin over us by putting our sins to death on his cross. This is how our Messiah will save us: not by military victories, but by taking on our defeats and becoming a "loser" to make winners out of us!

Our **gospel** has already appeared and been discussed in the Mass of December 21st (please read p. 45). It chronicles the first moment of recognition between precursor and savior, the beginning of their partnership in God's saving work for his people. Since Elizabeth is "filled with the Holy Spirit," she is able to interpret the event theologically. And her praise of Mary is not for her thoughtfulness in coming to aid her, but for her loyal obedience to God's offer. It's not just family warmth that Luke points out, but the saving work of God on our behalf. And just think, it's just about to start!

VIGIL OF CHRISTMAS
A-B-C Scripture

Isaiah 62:1-5 *Nations shall behold your vindication; / you shall be called by a new name. / No more shall men call you "Forsaken," / but "My Delight." / For the LORD delights in you / and makes your land his spouse. / As a bridegroom rejoices in his bride / so shall your God rejoice in you.*

Responsorial Psalm 89: 4-5, 16-17, 27, 29

Acts 13:16-17, 22-25 *Fellow Israelites and you others who are God-fearing, the God of Israel chose our ancestors and with uplifted arm he led them out. Then he raised up David as their king; from this man's descendants God, according to his promise, has brought to Israel a savior, Jesus. John heralded his coming by proclaiming a baptism of repentance to all the people of Israel.*

Matthew 1:1-25 *The book of the genealogy of Jesus Christ, the son of David, the son of Abraham. Now this is how the birth of Jesus Christ came about. When his mother Mary was betrothed to Joseph, but before they lived together, she was found with child through the Holy Spirit. The angel of the Lord appeared to him in a dream and said, "Joseph, son of David, take Mary your wife into your home. She will bear a son and you are to name him Jesus, because he will save his people from their sins."*

Reflection:

Jerusalem will receive a glorious restoration after her people return from Babylonian captivity. "Nations shall behold your vindication... you shall be called by a new name [signifying a whole new startover]... no more shall men call you 'Forsaken,' but you shall be called 'My Delight,' for the Lord delights in you, and makes your land his spouse." When Jesus is born as one of us, God is linking himself so intimately to us, that it's as if he were marrying mankind. "As a bridegroom rejoices in his bride, so shall your God rejoice in you."

Along his missionary journeys, Paul always visited his Jewish brethren first, hoping to make contact with their faith and lead them to see Jesus as the promised Christ they all longed for. At the synagogue in Antioch he briefly but engagingly covers the history of God's saving efforts for his people, leading up to Jesus as David's royal heir, recognized and announced by the Baptist as the fulfillment of all those Old Testament promises of renewed greatness that kept the hearts of all those Jews, dispersed throughout the Mediterranean, anchored firmly in Jerusalem. The Gospel of Matthew is the most Jewish of all, aimed primarily at converts from Judaism, exposing and exploring all the connections between O.T. hopes and their coming to fruition in the person of Jesus, the Christ, the long-awaited Messiah. Three times in this 25-verse selection he calls Jesus "Christ/Messiah," at the start and at the end of the genealogy, and at the introduction to his birth story.

Scripture scholars assure us that the neat subdivision into 14's was an artifice: it turns out that when the Aramaic letters for "David" are rendered as numbers, they total 14! So Matthew pulls the entire history of his people, from patriarchs to kings to the nobodies who returned from Babylon (their names appear nowhere else in the Scriptures), into his presentation of the Christ. The strange patriarchal choices of God, who prefers, as ancestors of the Messiah, cheats and liars (Jacob and Judah) to more rudely honest figures (as Esau or Joseph), will be echoed in Jesus' surprising choices of humble sinners over the (self-proclaimed) just who distance themselves from the physically and/or morally unfit. And as for nobodies: how about the band of apostles Jesus picked as his inner group? Turns out there's room—and hope—for us all.

CHRISTMAS MIDNIGHT MASS
A-B-C Scripture

Isaiah 9:1-6 *The people who walked in darkness / have seen a great light. / For a child is born to us, a son is given us; / they name him Prince of Peace. / His dominion is vast / and forever peaceful. / The zeal of the LORD of hosts will do this!*

Responsorial Psalm 96: 1-2, 2-3, 11-12, 13
Titus 2:11-14 *The grace of God has appeared, saving all and training*

us to live temperately, justly, and devoutly in this age, as we await the blessed hope, the appearance of the glory of the great God and of our savior Jesus Christ, who gave himself for us to deliver us from all lawlessness and to cleanse for himself a people as his own, eager to do what is good.

Luke 2:1-14 *In those days a decree went out from Caesar Augustus that the whole world should be enrolled. Joseph went up from Nazareth to Bethlehem, to be enrolled with Mary, his betrothed, who was with child. While they were there, she gave birth to her firstborn son. Now there were shepherds in that region living in the fields and keeping the night watch over their flock. The angel of the Lord appeared to them and the glory of the Lord shone around them, and they were struck with great fear. The angel said to them, "Do not be afraid; for behold, I proclaim to you good news of great joy that will be for all the people. For today in the city of David a savior has been born for you who is Messiah and Lord.*

Reflection:

Light shines out of the gloom of darkness, bringing abundant joy and great rejoicing. A child is born to us, the Prince of Peace, and all the instruments of war will be burned, producing light and warmth instead of devastation. Seems unlikely? Isaiah assures us that "the zeal of the Lord of hosts will do this!"

Our responsorial psalm invites all creation to join in the praises of our saving God. "Let the heavens be glad and the earth rejoice; let the sea and what fills it resound; let the plains be joyful and all that is in them!" And why do the trees of the forest exult? Because the Lord "comes to rule the world with justice." All will be well; our salvation is here; the Lord himself will set things straight.

Paul assures Titus that even as the grace of God has appeared, offering salvation to all, we must live "temperately, justly, and devoutly in this age as we await our blessed hope, the appearing of the glory of the great God and of our Savior Christ Jesus." The first, humble coming of Christ prepares us for his glorious Second Coming, as he cleanses for himself "a people of his own, eager to do what is right." What a beautifully encouraging prospect: not only are we called to closeness to God, we are by his grace made eager to come ever closer!

Luke's Gospel provides a richly detailed account of the birth of Jesus, how God arranged for him to come to his royal Messianic ancestor David's hometown, to be born not in a palace but a barn, welcomed not by the court but by shepherds gathered by angels calling them and singing the praises of God. God is faithful to his promises: through this Child he will look after his people, especially the little ones, the poor, sinners, the cast-aside. A grace-filled light now shines on us in the darkness of our sin-filled past. What a present is his presence! *Merry Christmas!*

CHRISTMAS DAWN
A-B-C Scripture

Isaiah 62:11-12 *The LORD proclaims: / Say to daughter Zion, your savior comes! / They shall be called the holy people, / the redeemed of the LORD, /and you shall be called "Frequented," / a city that is not forsaken.*

Responsorial Psalm 97: 1, 6, 11-12

Titus 3:4-7 *When the kindness and generous love of God our savior appeared, not because of any righteous deeds we had done but because of his mercy, he saved us through the bath of rebirth and renewal by the holy Spirit, whom he richly poured out on us through Jesus Christ our savior, so that we might be justified by his grace and become heirs in hope of eternal life.*

Luke 2:15-20 *When the angels went away the shepherds said to one another, "Let us go, then, to Bethlehem to see what has taken place." So they went in haste and found Mary and Joseph, and the infant lying in the manger. And Mary kept all these things, reflecting on them in her heart.*

Reflection:

This morning's selection from Isaiah is brief but to the point. "Say to daughter Zion," he is charged, "your Savior comes!" As for the people returning penniless and nearly hopeless from Babylon to their ruined, practically abandoned city, "they shall be called the holy people, the redeemed of the Lord, and you shall be called 'Frequented,' a city that is not [any longer] forsaken."

As God had made clear to the returning exiles, Paul reminds his readers that they've been redeemed, not by any righteous deeds on their part, but by the loving kindness of God through the gift of baptism. Hey, it's Christmas! What did you get? The Spirit, "lavished on us through Jesus Christ our Savior, that we might be justified by his grace," so that we are made heirs, with Jesus, of God's own eternal life! Wow, what a gift! The Gospel recounts how the shepherds, having received the angelic announcement, decide to go check it out, and find the Holy Family, with the Infant wrapped in swaddling clothes, just as they had been told. And they returned, glorifying and praising God.

Mary takes it all in—over time, she'll revisit the event with ever greater understanding, even as her faith is put to ever greater tests. Why didn't God provide any place for her baby to be born indoors, safe and snug? What was he doing leaving home and wandering around with these strange friends of his? Couldn't he see he was getting into ever-deeper trouble with the authorities? How could the people have asked for a hardened criminal to be released and for her son to be crucified? What could God possibly have in mind with all this? "Mary treasured all these things, and reflected on them in her heart," even as she stood at the foot of the Cross. Yes, our Savior has come, and we have been redeemed—but at a great price. How great must be the love of the Father for us!

CHRISTMAS DAY
A-B-C Scripture

Isaiah 52:7-10 *Your watchmen shout for joy, for they see the LORD restoring Zion.*

Responsorial Psalm 98:1, 2-3, 3-4, 5-6

Hebrews 1:1-6 *In times past, God spoke in partial and various ways to our ancestors through the prophets; in these last days, he spoke to us through a son, through whom he created the universe, who is the very imprint of his being, and who sustains all things by his mighty word.*

John 1:1-18 *In the beginning was the Word, and the Word was with God, and the Word was God. All things came to be through him, and to those who did accept him he gave power to become children of God, born not by natural generation but of God. And the Word became flesh and made his dwelling among us, and we saw his glory, the glory as of the Father's only Son.*

Reflection:
The watchmen on Jerusalem's walls raise a cry and shout for joy, because they see God returning to rebuild his city, "announcing peace, bearing good news, announcing salvation." In the second reading we're assured that Jesus is the reflection of the Father's glory, in fact, "the exact representation of the Father's being." So from our New Testament perspective, we see the Father at work when Jesus comforts,

teaches, and heals. In the coming of Jesus as one of us, the super-human, transcendent Yahweh-in-the-sky has come close to us in a wonderful, approachable way, in his Son.

There is a remarkable evolution (I was about to say "progression," but it's really a "re-gression") in the placement of Jesus into our history by his chroniclers. Mark, the no-nonsense reporter of Jesus' activities, begins with the start of his public ministry (1:9), showing up at the Jordan and asking John to baptize him, initiating his career as itinerant preacher, which begins immediately after the arrest of John.

Matthew, aiming to convince his fellow Jews, legitimizes Jesus by trac-ing him down, from the very source of all things Jewish, Abraham the Patriarch (1:1), to Joseph, the husband of Mary, "of her was born Jesus who is called Christ." Luke is the Gentile, ever the universalist, so he doesn't center on Abraham, but traces Jesus upwards from Joseph, son of Heli (3:23), all the way back to "Adam, son of God." Cute.

To sum up, then: Mark presents Jesus in medias res, commissioned at his baptism by the Father's recognition and approval, empowered by the Holy Spirit to begin his saving work. Matthew roots Jesus in Jewish history by tracing his descent from Abraham. Luke roots Jesus in human history by tracing his lineage all the way back to Adam. Now John comes, the maverick, the non-Synoptic, and puts Jesus outside of history, with God the Father since before creation. In fact, it was through him that "all things came into being."

As the Word (Greek: logos) he is the outward expression of God's transcendence. He is, after all, the "exact representation of the Father's being." In the light of his humanity we see a distant God, otherwise beyond the reach of our vision, now revealed as a loving Abba for Jesus, who by his entry into our human family, makes him the Abba of us all! Merry Christmas!

FEAST OF THE HOLY FAMILY

(SUNDAY IN THE OCTAVE OF CHRISTMAS)

A-B-C Scripture

Sirach 3:2-6, 12-14 *The LORD sets a father in honor over his children; a mother's authority he confirms over her sons. My son, take care of your father when he is old. Even if his mind fail, be considerate with him. For kindness to a father will take lasting root.*

Responsorial Psalm 128: 1-2, 3, 4-5

Colossians 3:12-21 *Put on then, as God's chosen ones, heartfelt compassion, kindness, humility, gentleness, and patience, bearing with one another and forgiving one another, as the Lord has forgiven you. And over all these put on love, that is, the bond of perfection. And let the peace of Christ control your hearts, and be thankful, singing psalms, hymns, and spiritual songs with gratitude in your hearts to God. And whatever you do, in word or in deed, do everything in the name of the Lord Jesus, giving thanks to God the Father through him. Wives, be subordinate to your husbands, as is proper in the Lord. Husbands, love your wives, and avoid any bitterness toward them. Children, obey your parents in everything, for this is pleasing to the Lord. Fathers, do not provoke your children, so they may not become discouraged.*

Reflection:

Sirach lists the socially expected behaviors of members of a family according to the Greco-Roman world of the second century before Christ. Parents are set up over children by the authority of God, and therefore are due our respect and care. Particularly tender (and timely) is the admonition to "take care of your father when he is old…even if his mind fail, be considerate with him; revile him not in the fullness of your strength." And of course, your treatment of your parents is ideally the school for your children's future behavior toward you.

Paul gives the Christians at Colossus an endearing catalog of domestic virtues: mercy, kindness, patience, forgiveness, and "over all these virtues put on love, which binds the rest together and makes them perfect." The call for wives to be submissive to their husbands is not unilateral; husbands are called to love their wives—which means (for those who pattern their lives on Christ) that they must put the welfare of their wives (and children) ahead of their own, and do good to them, whether they are thanked for it, get anything out of it for themselves, or enjoy it. And once again we find a tender touch: "do not nag your children lest they lose heart."

Cycle A – Gospel

Matthew 2: 13-15, 19-23 After the Magi ended their visit, an angel warned Joseph to take his family to safety in Egypt, since Herod was after the child to destroy any threat to his rule. After Herod dies, Joseph returns, *"Out of Egypt I have called my son."* Warned in another dream, he decides to bypass Judea, where Herod's son Archelaus rules, and heads for the region of Galilee, to a town called Nazareth. *"He shall be called a Nazarean."*

Reflection:
Even the Holy Family, during the infancy of Jesus, is called upon to suffer along with him. They are persecuted, become refugees/displaced persons, attempt to return home but can't, then settle for the safety of the north, away from Judea and Jerusalem's politics. Even in these vicissitudes, good old Matthew finds it possible to work in not one but two instances of fulfilled prophecies about this promised Child who will become the Messiah.

Cycle B – Gospel

Luke 2: 22-40 (shorter 2: 22, 39-40) The day comes for the parents of Jesus to present him at the Temple, since *"Every first-born male shall be consecrated to the Lord"* [remember Exodus?]. A just and pious elder, Simeon, now comes into the picture, takes the child in his arms, and blesses God: *"Now, Master, you can dismiss your servant in peace; you have fulfilled your word. For my eyes have witnessed your saving deed displayed for all the peoples to see: a revealing light to the Gentiles, the glory of your people Israel."* Coming on the scene at this moment, the prophetess Anna, a Temple regular, joins in thanking God and talks about the child to all who look forward to the deliverance of Jerusalem.

Reflection:

I'm sure they had no clue of all this public recognition of their little child as the long-promised Savior. First Simeon, the holy old man who sees the fulfillment of God's promise that he would not die without setting eyes on the Messiah to come. Then, a little Title IX, the respected prophetess Anna, who just about lived in the Temple since becoming a widow long before. She also is extended the privilege of recognizing this child and his role for his people. Now, as they return home, they have many years of quiet, ordinary living—but with lots to ponder in their hearts!

Cycle C – Gospel

Luke 2:41-52 *When he was twelve years old, they went up according to festival custom. As they were returning, the boy Jesus remained behind in Jerusalem, but his parents did not know it. They journeyed for a day and looked for him among their relatives and acquaintances, but not finding him, they returned to Jerusalem to look for him. After three days they found him in the temple, and his mother said to him,*

"Son, why have you done this to us?" And he said to them, "Why were you looking for me? Did you not know that I must be in my Father's house?" His mother kept all these things in her heart.

Reflection:
In today's Gospel Jesus is surprisingly causing his parents anguish, of all things! On one of their yearly visits to Jerusalem to celebrate the Passover (good family custom) he stays behind to join a group of teachers in discussion. "How could you do this to us? How could you cause us this sorrow?" "Where else would I be but in my Father's house?" Ouch. Mary keeps "all these things" to ponder in her heart. Our love for God the Father is paramount. Nothing can stand between his call and our response. And his love for us—to the point of making us his children—is the basis for all human relationships.

SOLEMNITY OF MARY, MOTHER OF GOD

(JANUARY 1ST)

A-B-C Scripture

Numbers 6:22-27 *The LORD said to Moses: "Tell Aaron and his sons: This is how you shall bless the Israelites: The LORD bless you and keep you! The LORD let his face shine upon you, and be gracious to you! The LORD look upon you kindly and give you peace! So shall they invoke my name upon the Israelites, and I will bless them."*

Responsorial Psalm 67: 2-3, 5, 6, 8

Galatians 4:4-7 *God sent his Son, born of a woman, born under the law, to ransom those under the law, so that we might receive adoption. As proof that you are children, God sent the spirit of his Son into our*

*hearts, crying out, "Abba, Father!" So you are no longer a slave but a
child, and if a child then also an heir, through God.*

Luke 2:16-21 *When eight days were completed for his circumcision,
he was named Jesus, the name given him by the angel before he was
conceived in the womb.*

Reflection:
How appropriate that the first reading on the first day of the new year
brings us Yahweh's order to Moses, to teach his brother Aaron and his
sons (the priestly tribe) just how they are to bless the people in his
name. In other words, these are the tools of the trade for my priests.
"So shall they invoke my name upon the Israelites, and I will bless
them." Don't we all at some time(s) in our prayer life get the feeling
that God has turned his face away from us and isn't listening? "The
Lord let his face shine upon you!" And we must remember that when
the God of the Hebrews said shalom he meant the richness of the
Hebrew concept: every good thing in full measure.

Paul details the coming of God's Son, "born under the law," born of a
woman, that is, fully human, one of us, sharing in our weakness, and
also in our subjection to the law. It is a sweet irony that Jesus becomes
subject to the law precisely so that he can lead us out from under it!
"Just what do you think you are—above the law?" "Well, ahem, now
that you mention it…yes." To be raised from the status of a slave to the
privilege of a child and heir is quite a promotion! The good news that
Jesus brings is that God does not demand a legal relationship from us,
he desires a parent-child relationship! By our adoption at baptism, the
Spirit in our hearts enables us to cry out "Abba" to the ever glorious
and awesome Lord God.

Our gospel is the same as the one used for the Christmas Mass at
Dawn, with the interesting addition of one last line, to prove that Jesus
was kosher, circumcised as required by Mosaic law. Yet this baby will
grow up to challenge the scribes and Pharisees and experts of the law

unabashedly (e.g. Matthew 23:13-26, esp.23-24). My favorite show-down is Mark 3:1-6 when "they watched him closely to see if he would cure on the Sabbath, so they might accuse him," and he asked them, "Is it lawful to do good on the Sabbath?...but they remained silent." So, angry and "grieved at their hardness of heart," he heals the man's withered hand right before their eyes, and they respond by immediately going out and plotting his death!

Jesus teaches us to become the kind of people for whom laws are unnecessary; we should understand that it is more important to answer the call to do good than to worry about the law. We are called, not to ignore the law, but to go beyond it to true Godly behavior. After all, we are God's children, not his slaves.

EPIPHANY OF THE LORD
(Sunday between 2 – 8 January)
A-B-C Scripture

Isaiah 60:1-6 *Rise up in splendor! Your light has come, / the glory of the Lord shines upon you. / Nations shall walk by your light; / they all gather and come to you. / The wealth of nations shall be brought to you. / Caravans of camels shall fill you, / bearing gold and frankin-cense, / and proclaiming the praises of the LORD.*

Responsorial Psalm 72: 1-2, 7-8, 10-11, 12-13

Ephesians 3:2-3, 5-6 *The mystery was made known to me by revela-tion, that the Gentiles are co-heirs, members of the same body, and co-partners in the promise in Christ Jesus through the gospel.*

Matthew 2:1-12 *When Jesus was born in Bethlehem of Judea, in the days of King Herod, magi from the east arrived in Jerusalem, saying,*

*"Where is the newborn king of the Jews? We saw his star at its rising
and have come to do him homage." Herod called the magi secretly
and ascertained from them the time of the star's appearance and sent
them to Bethlehem. The star preceded them, until it stopped over the
place where the child was. Entering the house they saw the child with
Mary his mother. They prostrated themselves and did him homage. Then
they opened their treasures and offered him gifts of gold, frankincense,
and myrrh.*

Reflection:

In Greek epiphany means: a making manifest, a revelation by sudden
insight, a bringing out into the light. And in just the first few verses
from Isaiah we hear of splendor, light, shining, radiance. This, God
will show us when we see not just the Israelites returning from Babylonian Captivity, but also the wealth of the nations (the Gentile world)
arriving in caravans of loaded-down camels "bearing gold and frankin-
cense, and proclaiming the praises of the Lord." What a welcome sight
that will be, when our God makes himself known to all the world and
they come here to Jerusalem, not to beat us up and carry us off, but to
join us in prayer and celebration.

And the gospel presents the wonderful fulfillment of this promised
event. Their image of wise seers from the mysterious East is like our
cartoon of the wizened old Tibetan monk seated on the mountaintop,
approached for answers by Westerners seeking his wisdom. It's one of
the Bible's gentle ironies that the Gentiles turn out to be more attentive
than the children of the promise to the approach of their Saving King.
Micah 5:1 provides the location of the birthplace—Bethlehem, David's
humble city, will welcome the Messiah. (Hmmm…kind of makes you
wonder what sort of Messiah this will be…will he enter Jerusalem
astride a high-stepping, noble steed? Hint: Eee-haw!)

Paul's letter to the Christians at Ephesus returns to the universality of Isaiah's vision: God's light reaches to all the world, and reveals the error of our ways when we divide people into the chosen and the excluded, the intimates of God (then: the Jews, now: Catholics, of course) and the rest of misguided, unfortunate mankind (then: Gentiles, now: non-Catholics…how easy!). Turns out God is revealing his Son as Savior of all, since he makes us all (gays and straights, street people and wage-earners, our kind and those who are "not our kind") members of the same body, the Church, the living Christ.

So this "unknown mystery" was not meant to be a secret—it was just too good to be believed, until Jesus came to make a demonstration (epiphany) of how it could work. With God there is no "us" and "them," much less an "us vs. them." We're all God's children, whether we know it or not. The shame of it is that there are so many people who still don't know it.

Is it just "too bad"? Or is it our obligation—now that we've seen the light—now that we've heard the word—to make sure we show our gratitude by bringing others out of their darkness of suspicion and fear into God's wonderful light, where all can see each other as brothers and sisters? We believe our God doesn't recognize any of our human distinctions and separations, that he won't even let our sins separate us from him, since Jesus dies for us while we are still in sin. How will people believe our God will come close to them if we don't? And how real is our gratitude to God if we don't go to others as he has come to us?

BAPTISM OF JESUS

(FLOATER: SUNDAY AFTER JANUARY 6TH,

UNLESS PRE-EMPTED BY

EPIPHANY—THEN IT'S ON NEXT DAY)

A-B-C Scripture

Isaiah 42:1-4, 6-7 *Here is my servant whom I uphold, / my chosen one with whom I am pleased, / upon whom I have put my spirit; / he shall bring forth justice to the nations. / I, the LORD, have called you for the victory of justice, / I have grasped you by the hand; / I formed you, and set you as a covenant of the people, / a light for the nations, / to open the eyes of the blind, / to bring out prisoners from confinement, / and from the dungeon, those who live in darkness.*

Responsorial Psalm 29: 1-2, 3-4, 9-10

Acts 10:34-38 *God shows no partiality. In every nation whoever fears him and acts uprightly is acceptable to him. This is the "good news of peace" proclaimed through Jesus Christ who is Lord of all. I take it you know about Jesus of Nazareth, beginning in Galilee with the baptism John preached, how God anointed him with the Holy Spirit and power.*

Reflection:

This pivotal event in the life of Jesus marks his commissioning by the Father and his empowerment by the Spirit to launch out, from a hidden life of preparation, to his public life of preaching the Good News of God's coming Kingdom. His career as Messiah begins at this moment. In this passage from the first of Isaiah's four "Songs of the Suffering Servant" the Church has always recognized Jesus as the one grasped by the hand, formed and set "as a covenant of the people, a light for the nations," sent by God "to open the eyes of the blind."

We don't know if Isaiah had an individual in mind, likely a king in their future, who must suffer much in his fidelity to God, or whether he was speaking in terms of the whole people of God serving as a pointer for the Gentile world. But we do know it fits Jesus perfectly, and in fact he will apply these texts to himself.

Peter's preaching in the house of the centurion Cornelius in a city named after Caesar (just how Gentile can a setting get?—a Roman official in a city named for an emperor) acknowledges God's acceptance of <u>anyone</u> who "fears him and acts uprightly." Peter realizes (with an assist from the vision he's received just before he comes downstairs to speak) that Jesus is "Lord of all, beginning in Galilee after [his] baptism," when "God anointed [him] with the Holy Spirit and power."

Cycle A – Gospel

Matthew 3: 13-17 *Jesus appeared before John at the Jordan to be baptized by him. John [protested], "I should be baptized by you, yet you come to me!" After Jesus was baptized, he came directly out of the water. Suddenly the sky opened and he saw the Spirit of God descend like a dove and hover over him. With that, a voice from the heavens said, "This is my beloved Son. My favor rests on him."*

Reflection:

Matthew's account points to Jesus' solidarity with us. Over his cousin's protests he insists on this passage-from-sin ceremony, though he is sinless, because he's doing it for us; his whole life is lived as God-WITH-us. Matthew also changes Mark's report: "You are my beloved Son" (a personal confirmation of Jesus' role), to: "This is my beloved Son," a message now addressed for <u>all</u> to hear, commissioning Jesus as his heaven-sent Messiah.

Cycle B – Gospel

Mark 1: 7-11 *Jesus came and was baptized in the Jordan by John. Immediately on coming up out of the water he saw the sky rent in two and the Spirit descending on him like a dove. Then a voice came from the heavens: "You are my beloved Son. On you my favor rests."*

Reflection:

Mark's is the pioneer gospel—the others would use his as at least a guide, and often as a source for their material. He chooses to present this scene as an audio-visual aid for his listeners. Jesus will hear the Father's mighty approbation and at the same time will see the Spirit descending on him in the form of a dove—the symbol of peace. He comes at God's behest to bring us God's kingdom of peace!

Cycle C – Gospel

Luke 3:15-16, 21-22 *After Jesus had been baptized and was praying, heaven was opened and the holy Spirit descended upon him in bodily form like a dove. And a voice came from heaven, "You are my beloved Son; with you I am well pleased."*

Reflection:

John the Baptist's baptism with <u>water</u> was the symbol used for inclusion of Gentile converts coming into Judaism—they had not yet crossed from sin and slavery (Egypt) into the homeland of freedom and righteousness promised to God's chosen as Moses led them through the <u>waters of the Red Sea</u>. Now John is calling Jews, already saved and assured of Yahweh's choice, to admit their sins and to reform <u>interiorly</u> so as to match their <u>external</u> observance of the Law. Jesus will segue seamlessly with his entire Messianic mission of getting his people to surpass the Law instead of being slaves to its limitations.